Legal, Effective
References

Practical HR

Legal, Effective References

How to Give and Get Them

Wendy Bliss, J.D., SPHR
Society for Human Resource Management
Alexandria, Virginia
USA
www.shrm.org

This publication is designed to provide accurate and authoritative information regarding the subject matter covered. It is sold with the understanding that neither the publisher nor the author is engaged in rendering legal or other professional service. If legal advice or other expert assistance is required, the services of a competent, licensed professional should be sought. The federal and state laws discussed in this book are subject to frequent revision and interpretation by amendments or judicial revisions that may significantly affect employer rights and obligations with respect to reference-checking activities. Readers are encouraged to seek legal counsel regarding specific policies and practices in their organizations.

This book is published by the Society for Human Resource Management (SHRM®). The interpretations, conclusions, and recommendations in this book are those of the author and do not necessarily represent those of SHRM.

The Society for Human Resource Management (SHRM) is the leading voice of the human resource profession, representing more than 160,000 professional and student members throughout the world. Visit SHRM Online at www.shrm.org.

Library of Congress Cataloging-in-Publication Data
Bliss, Wendy, 1955-
     Legal, effective references: how to give and get them / Wendy Bliss.
          p. cm.
Includes bibliographical references and index.
     ISBN 1-58644-010-1
          1. Employment references — Law and legislation — Unites States. 2. Employment references — United States. I. Title.
     KF3457.6.Z9 B59 2001
     658.3'112 — dc21

Printed in the United States of America.
10 9 8 7 6 5 4 3 2 1

To Gene,
my best reference for what's important in
life and love

Contents

List of Illustrations   iii
Acknowledgments   v
Introduction   1

Chapter 1   **Realities**   3
             Truth, or Consequences, in Reference Checking 3
             Reference Checking in Today's Workplace 4
             Reference-Checking Challenges and Opportunities 5
             A Reference "Reality Check" for Your Workplace 8

Chapter 2   **Legalities**   11
             The Reference-Checking Dilemma 11
             Test Your Knowledge 12
             Reference Risk 1: Providing Too Much Information 14
             Reference Risk 2: Not Providing Enough Information 22
             Reference Risk 3: Not Obtaining Enough Information 24
             Reference Risk 4: Obtaining Too Much Information 26
             State Laws 30
             International Laws 32

Chapter 3   **Practicalities: Giving References**   33
             The Balancing Act 33
             Out of Balance: Typical Approaches
                 to Giving References 33
             Achieving Balance: How to Decrease Legal Risks
                 while Providing Substantive References 36
             Handling Reference Inquiries 42
             23 Tips for Giving References 49

Chapter 4 Practicalities: Getting References Yourself　　**53**

Hide and Seek 53
Ask Me No Secrets and I'll Tell You No Lies 54
Ground Rules for Pre-employment Screening 55
What Additional Investigation Is Necessary 57
It's My Policy and I'm Sticking to It 60
Put It in Writing 63
I Get By with a Little Help from My Applicants 72
Calling All References 76
You've Got References—Now What? 85
30 Tips for Getting References 87

Chapter 5 Practicalities: Getting References with Help from the Pros　　**91**

Inside or Outside: Upsides and Downsides 91
The Choice Is Yours: Selecting the Right
　　Screening Firm 95
The Fair Credit Reporting Act 98

Chapter 6 Practicalities: Reference Checking in Your Organization　　**103**

A New Beginning for Your Reference-Checking
　　Program? 103
Taking a Second Look at Your Reference-Checking
　　Practices 104

Appendix A Answers to "Test Your Knowledge of Legal Issues," Chapter 2　　**111**

Appendix B References: A European Perspective　　**115**

Appendix C A Sample Listing of Firms Providing Pre-employment Screening Services　　**121**

Notes　　**125**

Index　　**127**

About the Author　　**133**

Illustrations

Figures

Figure 1.	The Four Corners of the Reference-Checking Dilemma	12
Figure 2.	Test Your Knowledge of Legal Issues	13
Figure 3.	Hiring Horror Stories	25
Figure 4.	Don't Ask, Don't Tell: 15 Questions That Spell "L-a-w-s-u-i-t"	28
Figure 5.	Sample Policy on Providing Employment References	37
Figure 6.	Sample Employee Consent to Disclose Personnel Information and Release of Liability	40
Figure 7.	Sample Record of Employee Reference Form	47
Figure 8.	Sample General Policy on Checking References for All New Hires	61
Figure 9.	Sample Applicant's Consent to Obtain Background Information and Release of Liability	65
Figure 10.	Sample Reference-Checking Form	67
Figure 11.	Sample Notice to Job Applicants	73
Figure 12.	The Ladder of Reference Inquiries	79
Figure 13.	Types of Services Provided by Pre-employment Screening Firms	94
Figure 14.	Seven "C-crets" for Selecting a Screening Firm	95
Figure 15.	Evaluating and Designing a Reference-Checking Program	104

Tables

Table 1.	States with Reference Immunity Laws	30
Table 2.	States with Blacklisting or Service-Letter Laws	32
Table 3.	Reference Information Regularly Provided when Requested	35
Table 4.	Falsified Information Found during Reference Checks	54
Table 5.	Reference-Checking Methods Compared	76
Table 6.	Internal vs. External Screening	92

Acknowledgments

Books don't write themselves, nor did I ever feel I was working alone on this one. Many people inspired, supported, and helped me to complete this book, and to each of them I offer sincere thanks and appreciation.

My editor, Laura Lawson, is a woman whose many positive attributes include her professional expertise, insightfulness, common sense, flexibility, and ability to nurture her authors. I cannot imagine a better editorial partner for my first book. Under Laura's sponsorship, this book moved smoothly from concept to publication in less than a year.

My new colleagues from the United Kingdom, solicitors Elizabeth Gillow and Martin Hopkins of Eversheds law firm in Birmingham, graciously shared their expertise on international issues in reference checking, and wrote Appendix B. A special "thank you" also is due to the professionals who reviewed the manuscript: Rosemary M. Collyer of Crowell & Moring LLP, who did a final legal review; Amy M. Maingault, PHR, Information Specialist in SHRM's Information Center; and Deborah Keary, SPHR, Director of the Information Center.

Several individuals provided valuable insider perspectives on the pre-employment screening services industry, including Chris Bailey, Director of Communications, Advantage Assessment Inc.; Paul W. Barada, President of Barada Associates, Inc.; Tony Raker, Vice President of Client Relations for American Background Information Services, Inc.; and Dean Suposs, Chief Executive Officer of Avert, Inc.

My affiliation with the Society for Human Resource Management (SHRM) in the past decade has been extremely rewarding personally and professionally, in large part because of the dedicated human resource professionals and the exceptional staff members I have had the opportunity to meet and work with.

I am particularly indebted to several SHRM staff members. Barbara Sadek and Nancy Woolever got the ball rolling on this book (and didn't even know it) when they asked me to speak, and keep speaking, on the topic of reference checking at SHRM national conferences and SHRM Employment Law and Legislative Conferences. Kristin Bowl and Angela Georgallis gave me many opportunities to spread the word on safe and sound reference practices to the members of the national and human resource press. Elizabeth Owens went above and beyond the call of duty to keep me informed and up to date on state legislation. Deron Zeppelin was a valuable resource for information on the Fair Credit Reporting Act.

The human resource professionals who have attended my reference-checking programs have been a wonderful source of information on real-world challenges and best practices in reference checking. Each of these experiences broadened and deepened my knowledge of the topic and allowed me to verify what was or was not working "in the trenches."

My family and in-laws have been beside me and behind me for this book, as they have for all my other professional endeavors. Their constant support of my dreams, and their tolerance of the countless hours I spend to achieve them, never ceases to amaze me.

My mother and my Aunt Edith were always willing, helpful listeners and encouragers as I worked my way through the writing process.

I owe a special debt of gratitude to my brother and mentor, Bryan, who was there to point me in the direction of the legal, human resource, and consulting professions, and to assist me along the way with his sound advice, gentle guidance, and tangible support.

Last, but always first, thanks to my husband and "in-house" lawyer, Gene, for his help at every phase of this project, including reviewing, editing, and proofing the manuscript and assisting with the development of the forms.

Legal, Effective References

Introduction

"Impossible." "Waste of time." "Litigation land mine." "Always ask, never tell." These are typical comments I've heard in the last several years from hundreds of human resources professionals and managers about reference checks. They reflect common frustrations experienced by reference-seekers and the general fear felt by reference-givers.

Reference checking has become a "hot button" issue employers face on a daily basis. How did such a seemingly simple, straightforward part of the hiring process become so challenging? In part, because of the increase in the number and types of lawsuits initiated since the 1980s relating to allegedly improper reference-checking practices. In part, because many employers have erected unnecessary barriers to the exchange of information about former employees or have engaged in ineffective pre-employment screening practices.

This book examines the two sides of the reference-checking equation— giving and getting—and how employers can implement workable solutions on both sides of this equation. You may be surprised to learn that you can add depth and substance when responding to reference requests about former and current employees while subtracting potential risks of legal liability; you also can multiply the benefits while dividing the burdens of obtaining references about job applicants.

The goal of this book is to make you, as employers, human resource professionals, executives, managers, or supervisors, aware of the increased importance of reference checking and to provide practical information that will enable you to handle this essential aspect of the hiring process both legally and effectively. Chapter 1 addresses the *realities* of reference checking in modern workplaces and within your organization. Chapter 2 focuses on the *legalities* of obtaining and providing references.

Chapters 3, 4, and 5 cover the *practicalities* of reference checking, including tips and techniques for giving references (Chapter 3) and getting references, either internally (Chapter 4) or with help from outside professionals (Chapter 5). Chapter 6 contains a worksheet you can use to evaluate and enhance your company's reference-checking program.

It is my hope that when you've finished this book, you won't use the statements above to describe reference checking, but will instead view reference checks as "indispensable," "well worth the time and effort," "an employer's gold mine," and "easy to do safely if you have sound policies and practices."

CHAPTER 1

Realities

Truth, or Consequences, in Reference Checking

Employers, beware. Hiring employees is a risky business. So, too, is talking about former employees to prospective employers. In either situation,
failure to get to the truth about applicants can lead to disastrous consequences. Consider these recent cases:

- In September 2000, a doctor admitted to murdering three patients at a
  veterans' hospital by lethally injecting them with poison. The Federal
  Bureau of Investigation suspected that the physician might have murdered up to sixty individuals during his medical career, which would
  make him one of the most prolific serial killers in history. Despite convictions on multiple counts of aggravated battery for poisoning
  coworkers, national television publicity about these convictions, and
  the loss of his medical license, the doctor was hired to serve on the
  medical staffs of several U.S. and foreign hospitals between 1987 and
  1997. Given these circumstances, how was he able to find employment
  as a medical caregiver? According to one of the medical centers where
  he worked, "Standard procedures for checking applicants were not followed."[1,2]

- A convicted embezzler who changed his name and concocted a work
  history as an Internet executive landed a position as the chief executive
  of a Southern California Internet start-up company. (He was later
  arrested when his true identity was discovered.) Similarly, the head of
  a well-known software development company resigned after a *Wall
  Street Journal* article uncovered embellishments of his education and
  other achievements. In a third case, the *San Francisco Chronicle* discovered some surprising facts about the cofounder and chief executive
  officer of a Northern California information systems company that

raised $26 million in venture capital. This entrepreneur, who claimed to have obtained degrees from Harvard and Columbia while he was working as many as four jobs, actually never graduated from these universities. His professional biography contained other discrepancies relating to his work history and activities as a professional soccer player. When chief executives falsify their credentials like these three individuals did, it can tarnish the reputation of their organizations as well.[3]

■ A high school teacher/administrator resigned under pressure at two schools following numerous allegations of his sexual misconduct with students. He was subsequently hired as a vice principal at a third school, where he was accused of sexually molesting a thirteen-year-old student. Several officials at the first two schools wrote glowing letters of recommendation for this individual. These letters contained numerous kudos about his "genuine concern" for students and "for making the campus . . . a safe, orderly, and clean environment for students" and described him as "an upbeat, enthusiastic administrator who relates well to the students." Unfortunately for his students and new employer, none of these references mentioned the numerous sexual improprieties or disciplinary actions taken against him.[4]

These cases vividly illustrate what can happen when employers do not take proper steps to verify, or do not provide accurate information about, an applicant's credentials and background. Exactly what steps are reasonable varies by the job, the organization, and the state in which a company is located; however, thorough reference checking should be a cornerstone of the employee selection process for every new hire.

Reference Checking in Today's Workplace

Reference checking is an important, but often frustrating, aspect of the hiring process. If done well, the reference-checking process helps employers both in screening "in" qualified candidates who are good fits for the job and the organization and in screening "out" incompetent or otherwise unsuitable individuals.

Most organizations check references and allocate significant resources to this activity. A 1998 survey by the Society for Human Resource Management (SHRM) found that more than 80% of employers polled conduct reference checks regularly for professional, executive, administrative, and technical positions. In addition, according to a study of employment managers at *Fortune 500* companies, approximately 10% of the time devoted to staffing is spent on reference checking.[5] Outsourcing may alleviate the frustrations of the process, but at a price. It may cost from as little as $10 to more than $100 per reference requested for each candidate, depending on the nature and extent of the reference check and the report provided.

In spite of the time and money spent on checking references, employers often experience difficulty in gathering more than "bare-bones" information about an applicant's track record. The findings of the 1998 SHRM reference-checking survey clearly illustrate this problem. This study revealed that while 91% of respondent employers were regularly able to obtain adequate information from former employers about candidates' dates of employment, less than one-third of these employers were regularly able to obtain sufficient information about candidates' qualifications, work habits, and reasons for leaving. Only 5% of employers in the SHRM survey could regularly obtain adequate information about candidates' violent or bizarre behaviors.

For more information about SHRM initiatives in reference checking, go to www.shrm.org and perform a search on the phrase "reference checking."

Reference-Checking Challenges and Opportunities

Employers face distinct challenges in getting and giving references, but have the potential to create distinct advantages with effective practices. Three key employer objectives in obtaining references are: 1) verifying information; 2) protecting the organization and its employees; and 3) avoiding legal problems associated with poor hiring decisions. Meeting these objectives will enable an employer to hire the best candidates, avoid hiring disasters, reduce costs, and increase productivity.

Verify Truth of Applicant Statements

In an ideal world, reference checking would be unnecessary because employers could rely on all statements made by applicants in résumés, employment applications, and interviews. In the real world, employers proceed at their peril if they fail to confirm what applicants tell them. The magnitude of deception that occurs during the hiring process is staggering. Numerous studies report that 25% to 40% of applicants provide false, exaggerated, or misleading information about their qualifications or backgrounds. One survey by Reid Psychological Systems even found that 95% of college students polled would lie to get a job, and that 41% of those students had already done so.

Prevent Problems Caused by Poor Hiring Decisions

Sound reference-checking practices can help organizations avoid two serious problems plaguing workplaces throughout the United States—workplace violence and employee theft. Consider these sobering facts:

- Approximately two million acts of violence occur in U.S. workplaces annually, according to a July 1998 report by the U.S. Department of Justice.

- Fifty-seven percent of human resource professionals responding to SHRM's 1999 Workplace Violence Survey reported that a violent incident or threat of such an incident had occurred in their organization between January 1996 and July 1999.

- Workplace violence costs American businesses an estimated $36 billion per year in medical care, counseling, and legal costs, according to a report of the Workplace Violence Research Institute.

- Ninety-five percent of U.S. businesses have been victims of fraud by trusted employees, reports American Background Information Services, Inc.

- Employee dishonesty costs businesses 1% to 2% of gross sales, according to the U.S. Chamber of Commerce.

While employers should take a variety of steps to reduce the threat of workplace violence and losses due to theft, one of the most critical steps is to use pre-employment screening techniques that enable companies to reject individuals who are prone to violence or dishonesty.

Moreover, by obtaining in-depth information about applicants' past job performance and work habits, employers are able to identify and reject individuals who are incompetent or have a history of discipline problems or chronic absenteeism. By ferreting out individuals who would be a poor fit for the job or the organization, employers can also reap rewards of increased productivity and reduced turnover.

Reduce the Risk of Legal Liability

Employers run the risk of lawsuits for negligent hiring if they fail to exercise reasonable care in investigating an applicant's background, and as a result, hire an unsuitable individual who harms others in a way that was foreseeable based on that person's background. These lawsuits can be quite costly. The average settlement in lawsuits for negligent hiring exceeds $1.6 million, according to American Background Information Services, Inc.; even larger awards are possible.

One of the ironic aspects of reference checking is that human resource professionals and managers—the very people usually tasked with the job of checking references—seem to spend as much effort in *not* giving in-depth responses to reference requests about former employees as they do in attempting to get useful references for their own hiring decisions. The "silence is golden" approach to providing references has definitely triumphed over an "available on request" philosophy. Why? Because litigation anxiety is alive and well in the reference-checking arena. According to the 1998 SHRM reference-checking study, 45% of employers have refused to provide information about former employees in response to reference requests for fear of being sued.

But is silence really golden? Consider the following benefits that can result from employers providing such information:

- Company outplacement programs are more effective when productive former employees' job search efforts are supported by in-depth references.

- Unemployment insurance premiums are reduced because the sooner unemployed former workers can find another job, the lower the former employer's unemployment tax rate will be.

- Former employees whose performance was good are rewarded with favorable references.

- Current employees understand that there are long-term rewards for strong performance and good conduct.

■ Other employers are alerted to potential employees who have documented poor performance, misconduct, or other problem behaviors.

Before throwing their hands up in despair at the futility of getting complete and accurate references or establishing a strictly "name, rank, and serial number" policy for giving references, employers should thoroughly examine the legal issues on both sides of the reference-checking equation. With a full understanding of these issues, employers can develop reference-check policies and procedures that will minimize exposure to lawsuits and maximize benefits to the organization.

A Reference "Reality Check" for Your Workplace

Take the following "reality check" to review the current state of your organization's reference-checking practices, procedures, and legal awareness. A cross-reference to the chapter in which the topic is discussed is included next to each question. Compare and contrast your practices with the practices recommended in this book.

Giving References

1. Are you aware of the potential legal risks for providing too much or too little information when responding to a reference request? (See Chapter 2.)

2. Does your organization provide references for employees who have left your organization? (See Chapters 2 and 3.)

3. What specific categories of information does your organization typically permit to be disclosed in response to reference inquiries? (See Chapter 3.)

4. What types of information does your organization not allow to be discussed in response to reference inquiries? (See Chapter 3.)

5. Who in your organization is permitted to respond to reference requests? (See Chapter 3.)

6. Do you obtain consent from the individual in question before giving references? If so, when and how is this consent obtained? (See Chapter 3.)

7. What controls does your organization have in place to ensure consistency and fairness in handling reference requests and to minimize legal risks? (See Chapter 3.)

8. What documentation, if any, does your organization require when references are provided? (See Chapter 3.)

9. Where are records relating to references provided kept? Who has access to these records? How long are these records retained? (See Chapter 3.)

Getting References

1. Are you aware of the potential legal risks of getting too much or too little information when obtaining references about prospective employees? (See Chapter 2.)

2. Does your organization require reference checks before an individual is hired? (See Chapters 2 and 4.)

3. What other pre-employment screening activities does your organization conduct for all new hires? (See Chapter 4.)

4. Does your organization conduct background checks for certain jobs? If so, for what jobs? What types of background checks are conducted? (See Chapters 4 and 5.)

5. What types of information does your organization typically seek in a reference check? (See Chapter 4.)

6. If your reference and background checks are conducted internally, who in your organization handles this responsibility? (See Chapter 4.)

7. If third parties complete your reference checks, how were these parties selected? (See Chapter 5.)

8. Do you obtain consent from the individual before checking his or her references? If so, when and how is this consent obtained? (See Chapter 4.)

9. Do you inform applicants of your reference-checking practices and procedures? If so, when and how do you do this? (See Chapter 4.)

10. Do you typically check references by telephone, mail, fax, e-mail, or in person? (See Chapter 4.)

11. Do you seek assistance from applicants in obtaining references? If so, how do you do this? (See Chapter 4.)

12. What techniques do you use to get useful, in-depth reference information from former employers? (See Chapter 4.)

13. What documentation, if any, does your organization require when references are checked? (Chapter 4.)

14. Where are records relating to references obtained kept? Who has access to these records? How long are these records retained? (See Chapter 4.)

CHAPTER 2

Legalities

The Reference-Checking Dilemma

The reference-checking process—on both sides—makes many human resource professionals and most employment attorneys nervous about the possibility of lawsuits by former employees or job candidates. The good news is that employers are rarely sued because of their reference-checking activities. Only 1% of those surveyed in the 1998 SHRM reference-checking study had been sued either for defamation or for negligent hiring related to their reference-checking activities. The bad news is that, while the probability of being sued for reference-checking practices may be low, the costs of being sued can be substantial. It can easily cost more than $15,000 to respond to even a frivolous claim and more than $100,000 to go to trial, regardless of the outcome. If an employer loses a lawsuit, damage awards of more than $1 million are not unheard of.

The reference-checking process can put employers in a "sued if you do, sued if you don't" predicament. Whether giving or getting references, organizations are vulnerable to lawsuits if the wrong quantity or quality of information is sought or disclosed. Here's the dilemma employers find themselves in. They may be sued not only for disclosing too much information in response to a reference request concerning a former employee, but also for not giving enough information to prospective employers. In addition, there are possible legal hazards both for not obtaining adequate background information about applicants and for getting too much of the wrong type of information about them.

The parameters of this reference-checking dilemma are illustrated in Figure 1. This dilemma has four "corners," in which varied legal claims for reference-checking activities can arise. Fortunately, employers can take certain steps to walk the fine legal lines and avoid liability for giving

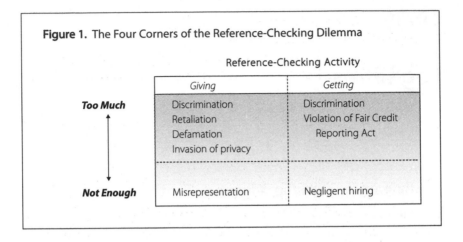

Figure 1. The Four Corners of the Reference-Checking Dilemma

Reference-Checking Activity

	Giving	Getting
Too Much	Discrimination Retaliation Defamation Invasion of privacy	Discrimination Violation of Fair Credit Reporting Act
Not Enough	Misrepresentation	Negligent hiring

or getting too much—or not enough—information during reference checks.

The best strategy for avoiding lawsuits in the reference-checking arena is to understand the potential legal pitfalls and implement prudent and effective reference-checking policies and procedures based on such knowledge. This chapter examines the legal aspects of reference checking. Chapters 3, 4, and 5 will offer practical guidance on how to give and get safe and effective job references.

Test Your Knowledge

The following true-false quiz (Figure 2, "Test Your Knowledge of Legal Issues") highlights some of the areas in which legal issues affect reference-checking practices. Answers and explanations appear in Appendix A.

Figure 2. Test Your Knowledge of Legal Issues

True/False

When giving a reference—

_____ 1. Employers have a duty to provide information about former employees' dates of employment, positions held, earnings, and job performances, upon request from any third party.

_____ 2. It is inadvisable to comment on the applicant's sexual preference unless specifically asked about it by the prospective employer.

_____ 3. As long as an employer provides only positive information about former employees, it can avoid potential legal liability.

_____ 4. In certain situations, an employer will not be liable for defamation when a supervisor makes false statements about a former employee.

_____ 5. Employers should not provide references for former employees who have filed discrimination claims.

When checking an applicant's reference—

_____ 6. Employers do not have to conduct the same number of reference checks for all candidates for the same position.

_____ 7. Employers have a duty to make a reasonable investigation of an individual's background before hiring that person.

_____ 8. If a former supervisor reveals information relating to an applicant's current pregnancy during a reference check, the potential employer should document this information so that it can be used in discussing scheduling issues.

_____ 9. It is permissible to inquire whether a candidate has filed a charge of discrimination because such information is job related.

_____ 10. The Fair Credit Reporting Act (FCRA) requires that employers who handle reference and background checks internally must obtain an applicant's prior written consent.

Reference Risk 1: Providing Too Much Information

The logical starting point for examining the legal aspects of reference checking is with the traditional area of concern to most employers—giving references. You can stray out of bounds legally when responding by

- providing a discriminatory reference,
- giving a negative reference in retaliation,
- providing a defamatory reference, or
- disclosing private facts that should have been kept confidential.

In each of these situations, potential liability arises because references are given for an improper purpose or contain inappropriate content that the requester had no right or need to know.

Discrimination

A negative reference should never be given for discriminatory reasons. Providing a bad reference based on an employee's or former employee's race, religion, gender, national origin, age, or disability is impermissible under federal equal employment opportunity (EEO) laws, including Title VII of the Civil Rights Act of 1964, the Age Discrimination in Employment Act of 1967, and the Americans with Disabilities Act of 1990.[6] For example, it would be illegal for a supervisor to suggest that a former employee, who is sixty years old, would be unsuited for a job at another organization because that employee is "over the hill" and nearing retirement age. The same would be true where state statutes provide greater protections against discrimination than federal statutes; for example, in protections as to sexual orientation or marital status.

To avoid claims of disparate treatment discrimination, employers should also provide the same amount of detail on the same topics for each former employee, to the extent the employee has consented to such reference disclosures.

Retaliation

Managers unfamiliar with EEO laws may be tempted to "get even" when receiving a reference request regarding an employee who complained about the employer's or manager's practices. However, even a small dash of revenge ruins the reference-giving recipe. Providing a bad reference to strike back at an employee who asserts rights protected by law is a form of illegal retaliation ("Case in Point #1: The U.S. Supreme Court Says Retaliation and References Don't Mix").

Retaliation is perhaps the most dangerous form of discrimination an employer can engage in. Why? First, retaliation is, by definition, intentional discrimination. Second, retaliation is, by definition, malicious. Third, a finding of retaliation requires a jury to assess what was going on in a manager's mind. Fourth, retaliation claims are more likely to "go to the jury"—that is, to survive an employer's motion for summary judgment in a discrimination lawsuit.

Retaliation can encompass any adverse action taken against an employee who files a complaint, supports another employee's complaint, or otherwise opposes unlawful practices. It is not *what* is done that is important, but *why*. Often, retaliation occurs after an employee has com-

Case in Point #1

The U.S. Supreme Court Says Retaliation and References Don't Mix[7]

After being fired by Shell Oil Company, Charles Robinson, Sr., filed a discrimination charge with the Equal Employment Opportunity Commission (EEOC). Robinson alleged that he had been terminated because of his race.

While the EEOC charge was pending, Robinson applied for a position at another organization. The prospective employer contacted Shell for a reference. Subsequently, in a Title VII lawsuit, Robinson asserted that Shell provided an unfavorable reference in retaliation against him for having filed the EEOC charge. The federal district and appeals courts dismissed Robinson's case, ruling that Title VII anti-retaliation provisions apply only to current employees.

The U.S. Supreme Court disagreed with the lower courts' interpretations of Title VII. It held that the term "employee" as used in Title VII's anti-retaliation provisions included former employees. Consequently, Robinson could sue Shell for allegedly retaliatory references.

This decision makes it clear that employers should not use references to "get even" with an employee who has exercised his or her statutory right to file a discrimination claim. An employer is not prohibited from providing a negative reference about a discharged employee if that person has filed a discrimination charge against the employer; however, retaliation cannot be the motive for the negative reference.

plained about discrimination, but there are many other statutory bases for retaliation lawsuits. It is illegal to retaliate against an employee who exercises his or her rights under the following federal laws.

- Title VII of the Civil Rights Act of 1964
- Age Discrimination in Employment Act
- Americans with Disabilities Act
- Immigration Reform and Control Act
- Uniformed Services Employment and Reemployment Rights Act
- Family and Medical Leave Act
- Fair Labor Standards Act
- Equal Pay Act
- Employee Retirement Income Security Act
- National Labor Relations Act
- Occupational Safety and Health Act
- Employee Polygraph Protection Act

State fair employment practices statutes almost always contain similar anti-retaliation provisions. In addition, most states recognize an exception to the employment-at-will doctrine where the employer retaliates against the employee for exercising a right or duty protected by public policy.

If your organization has a policy, practice, or procedure for giving references, departing from it to the detriment of a former employee who filed an EEO charge will place your company at risk that he or she will file an EEO charge for unlawful retaliation.

Defamation

The legal issue in reference checking that employers seem to be most aware of, and most worried about, is defamation. This common law tort occurs when a person impugns the reputation of another person by publishing—verbally or in writing—false and injurious statements. (Common law means, simply, law that is created by judges on a case-by-case basis, and it is distinguished from statutes and regulations that are written prospectively to be applied whenever certain situations arise in the future. And a tort, broadly speaking, is a bad act that is legally actionable, but different from a mere breach of contract.)

Defamatory oral communications, such as statements made on the telephone or face to face, constitute slander. Defamatory written communications, including comments in recommendation letters or on reference forms, constitute libel.

Most defamation lawsuits in the employment context are based on disparaging statements made by employers giving bad references on former employees ("Case in Point #2: Reckless References"). In some

> **Defamation occurs if**
> 1) there is publication of
> 2) a false statement of fact
> 3) to third parties
> 4) that damages a person's reputation.

cases state courts have ruled that legally actionable, defamatory references also can result from "compelled self-publication" by the person defamed. (However, the majority of states do not recognize the concept of compelled self-publication as a permissible basis for a defamation lawsuit.) Compelled self-publication cases have arisen in situations where an employer discharges an employee and then gives the employee a false, defamatory reason for the termination. When such employees seek other work, and are asked in interviews or on job applications about the reason for leaving the previous employer, such employees are placed in the awkward position of either being compelled to repeat defamatory statements about themselves or not responding truthfully.

Fear of defamation lawsuits has probably been the main reason for the widespread adoption of "name, rank, and serial number" policies for responding to reference requests. Such policies permit disclosure of only the most basic information (for example, dates of employment, title, and salary) to prospective employers. Most human resource professionals and supervisors have been "Mirandized" by their company's employment attorneys when it comes to giving references; that is, they have been advised: "You have the right to remain silent. Anything you say may be used against you in a court of law. You have the right to an attorney ...." (The only part of the Miranda warnings the lawyers don't give is the option to have an attorney appointed for the accused employer if the employer can't afford one!)

Sadly, the bad guys win and the good guys lose when employers provide only "name, rank, and serial" style references or make no comments whatsoever. The real winners under these policies are the applicants who have a record of poor performance and misconduct in their previous jobs. The losers are all the employers who are unable to obtain the critical information about job candidates' qualifications and track records at oth-

Case in Point #2

Reckless References[8]

Some things are better left unsaid during reference checks. Inaccurate and inflammatory comments about former employees during reference inquiries may provide the basis for large awards in defamation lawsuits.

In one such defamation case, an insurance sales executive named Larry Buck was awarded $1.9 million in actual and punitive damages from his former employer. Why? Because various representatives of Buck's former employer stated, in response to inquiries by prospective employers and Buck's private investigator, that Buck was

- "Horrible in a business sense"
- "Untrustworthy"
- "Not always entirely truthful"
- "Guilty of padding his expense account"
- "A crook"
- "Paranoid"
- "Irrational "
- "Ruthless"
- "A Jekyll and Hyde person"
- "A classical sociopath"

The jury in this case found that these and other statements made about Buck were defamatory and not protected by qualified privilege because they were malicious and substantially untrue.

This case illustrates the importance of sticking to the facts when giving references and not providing any reference information with the intent to injure a former employee, either through a deliberate falsehood or with reckless disregard for the truth. Another lesson from this case is the importance of knowing to whom you are speaking when responding to reference requests. Failure to follow these guidelines can be very costly, as Buck's former employer learned.

er organizations and the good employees who cannot get their former employers to say anything positive about them.

While employers need to take precautions against providing defamatory responses to reference requests, adherence to a strict "name, rank,

Case in Point #3

A Test of Truth[9]

A former managerial employee of Wal-Mart Stores, Inc., learned that if an employer has truth on its side when disclosing the employee's reason for discharge, a defamation lawsuit is a waste of the employee's time.

The employee, Michael Irwin, was fired after refusing to participate in a drug rehabilitation program after testing positive for cocaine use in a mandatory drug test. Wal-Mart stated in Irwin's service letter that "results of a urinalysis revealed an unacceptable level of a controlled substance in his system."

Irwin sued Wal-Mart for defamation. The Missouri court of appeals affirmed the trial court's dismissal of Irwin's case because Wal-Mart's service letter had told the truth, and nothing but the truth, about Irwin's drug test. Although these cold, hard facts may have been damaging to Irwin's reputation and hindered his job search efforts, the truth was a complete defense to Irwin's accusation of defamation.

and serial number" or "no comment" policy may be overkill. Moreover, such a restrictive policy is likely to have a detrimental effect on an organization's unemployment compensation expenses, outplacement efforts, and employee relations. The bare-bones approach to giving references may be unnecessary if an organization keeps in mind the following defenses to claims of defamation.

Truth

Truth is an absolute defense to a defamation claim. Where an employer has convincing proof that information given by its representative about a former employee is true, it cannot be held liable for defamation, regardless of how damaging the reference is ("Case in Point #3: A Test of Truth"). Nevertheless, to further minimize the potential for defamation lawsuits, do not provide unfavorable, but truthful, references unless such references would be covered by qualified privilege and the employee has consented to the reference.

Qualified and Absolute Privileges

Employers and their agents are not liable for defamation in situations where they are protected by an "absolute" or "qualified" privilege.

Although state laws vary, most states recognize an absolute privilege for employers to make defamatory statements when participating in judicial, arbitration, or administrative proceedings. Accordingly, an employer would not be held liable for defamation for statements it makes about current or former employees in the context of such proceedings.

A qualified privilege is less comprehensive than an absolute privilege and will only protect employers from liability for defamation if certain conditions are met. State laws vary, but generally an employer has a qualified privilege to publish a defamatory statement to protect its own or another's interest, provided the publication is reasonably necessary and made in good faith, and the privilege is not abused. Consequently, an employer has a right to give a third party information about an employee, even if the information is disparaging, as long as giving the information helps the employer protect an important interest of the employer or a third party. The doctrine of qualified privilege extends to communications between former and prospective employers to discuss job applicants.

Qualified privilege may not be recognized where an employer has abused the privilege by making false statements maliciously, either knowing the statement is false or with reckless disregard to whether it is true or false; providing unfavorable references that are not based on direct personal observation, documentation or employee admissions; or publishing the statement to a person who does not have a legitimate need.

Here is a checklist for employers giving references to ensure that their references are protected by the qualified privilege.

- Is the reference being provided in response to a legitimate inquiry by a party who has a valid need to know the information?
- Does the employer know or reasonably believe that the information given is true?
- Is the information being disclosed in good faith, rather than for an improper, malicious purpose?

Consent

If there is anything in the law that is the equivalent of a bulletproof vest, employee consent is probably it. Several court cases have held that, if an applicant or employee has given consent to an organization to provide or obtain references, then the organization may not be held liable for defamatory statements made by the employer's representatives during reference checks. Every organization can take steps to protect itself against defamation claims by requiring job applicants and former employees to sign a written consent and release of liability. Sample reference authorization forms appear in Chapters 3 and 4.

In addition to these common law defenses, a majority of states have enacted laws providing employers with statutory immunity from civil liability for good-faith references, even if those references are defamatory. See the section on state laws for more information and a list of states with reference-checking immunity laws.

Invasion of Privacy

In addition to avoiding claims for defamation, employers must beware of potential liability for the tort of invasion of privacy. To avoid invasion-of-privacy lawsuits, employers need to make sure they don't disclose inappropriate confidential information.

A legally actionable invasion of privacy can occur during reference checks when the reference divulges embarrassing personal facts about a former or current employee that should have been kept secret. For example, it would not be a good idea to remark during a reference conversation, "And by the way, you might like to know that Susan had an affair with a married man,"

> **An invasion of privacy occurs if**
> 1) there is a public disclosure
> 2) of private facts (even if the facts were true)
> 3) that should have been kept secret *and*
> 4) the disclosure is objectionable to a reasonable person.

"John is gay and his lover has AIDS," or "Chris has an abusive spouse."

Facts about an individual's sexual orientation or sexual activities should not be shared in reference checks, unless such information relates to documented incidents of workplace sexual misconduct or harassment. Similarly, disclosure of medical conditions may trigger claims for invasion of privacy and disability discrimination.

Disclosures of personal information about an individual during a reference check do not constitute an invasion of privacy if

■ the information has already been made public (for example, it appears in criminal, court, or other public records, or the individual has shared the information with many people) or

■ the individual has consented to the disclosure of information.

The best strategy for avoiding invasion of privacy liability when giving references is this: In response to specific questions, provide only *job-related* information, regardless of what is being asked. Do not *volunteer* even job-related information about former or current employees unless it has been requested.

Reference Risk 2: Not Providing Enough Information

Perhaps the most surprising legal aspect of giving references is that what is *not* said during a reference check can provide the grounds for a lawsuit. Recent cases in some states suggest that when an employer gives a favorable reference about a former employee, but fails to reveal pertinent information about the person's known dangerous tendencies, the employer may be liable for the torts of intentional or negligent misrepresentation.

Misrepresentation

Generally, employers have no legal obligation to provide references, although certain information about former employees must be disclosed to prospective employers pursuant to state service letter statutes (discussed in this chapter) or industry-specific regulations. Nonetheless, when employers do give references, they have a duty not to misrepresent or conceal a former employee's qualifications or character if this would pose a foreseeable risk of harm to others. If a potentially dangerous individual is hired because of a favorable, but misleading, reference and then causes physical injury or other harm (such as theft, fraud, or vandalism) in his or her new position, the reference-giver may be held liable for the resulting damages.

It is the telling of "half-truths" that creates the risk of misrepresentation claims. Consequently,

Misrepresentation occurs if
1) a former employer provided a positive reference
2) but did not disclose information about the former employee's dangerous tendencies
3) even though the former employer knew that this person's dangerous tendencies posed a foreseeable risk of harm *and*
4) the former employee injures others on the new job.

Case in Point #4

A Killer Recommendation Letter[10]

In a tragic workplace incident, a recommendation letter turned into an instrument of death.

A mentally unstable employee named Calden exhibited dangerous and disruptive tendencies when he worked at Allstate Insurance Company, including taking a concealed weapon to work on more than one occasion, threatening female employees, and stating he was an alien from outer space. Nevertheless, as part of his agreement to resign, Allstate gave Calden a recommendation letter, signed by a vice president, which stated Calden's resignation was the result of a corporate restructuring and unrelated to his job performance. Calden presented this letter during an interview at Fireman's Fund Insurance Company, and Fireman's Fund relied on it in offering Calden a job.

When Calden was fired from Fireman's Fund for an unexcused absence, he shot and killed several Fireman's Fund employees (including his supervisor and the director of human resources) and then killed himself. Families of the victims sued Calden's former employer, Allstate, for negligent referral for providing an allegedly misleading letter of recommendation that Fireman's Fund relied on in hiring Calden.

This negligent referral lawsuit against Allstate was settled before it went to trial. This case vividly illustrates the dangers of providing positive, or even neutral, references for an employee who has exhibited dangerous tendencies at work.

there are clear but opposite ways to avoid liability for misrepresentation when providing references about former employees with harmful tendencies—either tell the whole truth or say nothing at all.

While some courts have ruled that an employer does not have a duty to share information about an employee's dangerous tendencies with potential employers, there are more than legal issues to consider. While a policy of providing no references, or only "name, rank, and serial number" may be the safest course of action from a litigation prevention standpoint, it may not be the best course of action from an ethical, practical, or business perspective. Ask yourself this: Would you prefer to be sued for defamation because you said too much about a dangerous former employee or that someone be injured or killed because you said too little?

To bring this issue even closer to home, ask yourself this: What would you want to tell a prospective employer about a potentially violent former employee if one of your loved ones worked for that employer?

When it comes to giving references about employees who have dangerous propensities, it is a good idea to seek professional advice. A good employment attorney can help to avoid the legal risks and a good industrial psychologist can help avoid repercussions from the potentially violent employee ("Case in Point #4: A Killer Recommendation Letter").

Reference Risk 3: Not Obtaining Enough Information

While the predominant force in employer reference-giving practices may be fear; the prevailing theme in getting references is frustration. Because of the widespread use of restrictive reference policies, it may seem like an exercise in futility to try to get meaningful information from previous employers about the job performance, qualifications, and workplace behaviors of potential hires. Yet even though it is often difficult or impossible to find out about an individual's suitability for hire during the typical reference check, employers must make the effort. Failure to do so dramatically increases the likelihood of staffing disasters and lawsuits for negligent hiring lawsuits.

Negligent Hiring

Organizations whose employees have committed crimes such as murder, rape, assault, theft, and arson or caused personal injury and property losses within the scope of their employment may be targets of lawsuits for negligent hiring by the victims of these wrongful acts. Usually, perpetrators of such crimes are not doing it for the first time (Figure 3, "Hiring Horror Stories").

Employers have the right to hire the best-qualified individuals.

> **Negligent hiring occurs if**
>
> 1) an employer hires an unfit individual who injures others, *and*
>
> 2) the employer did not make an adequate inquiry into the applicant's background
>
> 3) so it failed to discover facts that would have led to the applicant's rejection
>
> 4) because of the foreseeable risk of harm presented by having the applicant work in the particular position.

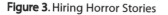

Figure 3. Hiring Horror Stories

When the wrong person slips through the hiring process, he or she can cause great harm. Consider the following real-life hiring horror stories.

- An Illinois detective agency hired a security guard, who raped and murdered an employee of one of the agency's clients after asking her to drive him to another work site. The guard had several misdemeanor convictions and an outstanding warrant for his arrest.

- An elderly visitor to a Texas nursing home was assaulted by an employee who was actually an unlicensed nurse previously convicted of fifty-six criminal offenses.

- A cook at an Orlando resort hotel who had a burglary and assault record raped a sixteen-year-old tourist in a hotel bathroom. The hotel was unaware of this employee's criminal record because it did not conduct background checks for cook positions.

- A Kansas City plumbing company hired a repairman, but since it did not conduct background checks, it did not discover that the employee had spent twenty-five years in prison for violent felonies including kidnapping, aggravated robbery, burglary, and assault. The repairman was sent to the home of an eighty-year-old widow, where he obtained $90 from her and left her home to buy crack cocaine with the money. He later returned and robbed and beat the elderly widow to death with a claw hammer.

These incidents are particularly distressing because in each case the violent employee had a history of dangerous conduct the employer might have discovered by conducting a criminal background check.

They also have a legal duty not to hire unfit individuals who pose a threat of harm to others. Employers may be liable for negligent hiring if they fail to make an adequate investigation into an applicant's background during the hiring process and, as a result, employ someone who harms a coworker, customer, or others.

The amount and type of investigation necessary to avoid claims of negligent hiring will vary by the position being filled. There is no one-size-fits-all test regarding the extent of the investigation an employer must undertake in every circumstance. Rather, the issue is one of reasonableness under the circumstances. Technological advances in information storage and retrieval permit today's managers to access a host of information about applicants with the press of a button. Correspondingly, prudent employers must conduct increasingly more sophisticated background investigations on job applicants. Employers should keep in mind that a jury is not likely to excuse an employer from doing a simple and inexpensive background check when doing so could have prevented great harm.

The scope of potential liability for negligent hiring is broad, and judicial standards as to what constitutes reasonable care in hiring are often difficult to articulate. Perhaps in response to such difficulties, some states have enacted laws in the area of negligent hiring. For example, Florida has passed a law providing safe harbor from liability for negligent hiring to employers that take one or more of five background-checking measures. Georgia, in contrast, has a statute that merely codifies the employer's duty to exercise "ordinary care in the selection of employees and not retain them after knowledge of incompetency."

Background checks are legally mandated for jobs in some industries. For instance, most states require a check for criminal convictions when hiring for positions involving working with minors. Some states also require a check for criminal convictions before hiring individuals as security guards, health care workers, or employees of a financial institution. Industries that have mandatory background check requirements include public education, transportation, and insurance.

Reference Risk 4: Obtaining Too Much Information

Although employers need to be diligent in learning about job candidates' backgrounds to minimize exposure to lawsuits for negligent hiring, they must not go overboard by seeking facts for which there is no legal need or right to know or by obtaining legitimate information through illegitimate means. If they do, they may violate discrimination laws or the federal Fair Credit Reporting Act (FCRA).

Discrimination

Intentional or inadvertent violations of federal discrimination laws or state fair employment practices statutes can occur during reference checks as a result of 1) the number of references contacted, 2) the types of questions asked, and 3) the way answers are used.

Reference-checking procedures should be consistent and based on legitimate business needs. While employers have discretion as to the number of references to be contacted for each candidate, the number of references contacted may be evidence of disparate treatment in a discrimination lawsuit. Consequently, as a general rule, the same number of references should be checked and the same questions asked at the same stage of the hiring process for all candidates applying for similar positions. For example, it would be discriminatory for a hospital nursing supervisor to check just one reference for female applicants and at least three references for male applicants applying for the same nursing positions. Variations from standard reference-checking procedures in the case of particular applicants should be based on documented, nondiscriminatory reasons. For example, an employer might wish to check more than the usual number of references if the employer receives contradictory information about a particular applicant.

It is acceptable to have different screening procedures for different jobs—as long as there is a sound business reason for the differences. For example, it would be appropriate for a hospital to contact more references for a health care worker position than for a cafeteria worker job because health care workers will be in frequent, unsupervised contact with patients.

Regardless of the job being filled, asking certain types of questions when checking references can violate discrimination laws. It is improper to ask questions about an applicant's race, gender, religion, national origin, age, disability, or other protected characteristics. A good rule of thumb for reference inquiries is: If you can't ask the question during an employment interview or on an application form, you can't ask the question during a reference check (Figure 4, "Don't Ask, Don't Tell").

In the real world, though, things often get more complicated. Even if you ask proper questions, that doesn't mean that you won't accidentally learn facts that you have no right to know. For instance, say you are doing a telephone reference check with the applicant's last supervisor. You ask a legitimate, nondiscriminatory question, such as, "How well did Sarah deal with stressful situations when she worked for you?" The former supervisor replies, "Not very well. Sarah suffers from manic depression. When we completed a company-wide reorganization last year and Sarah's job was restructured, she got so depressed that she often cried in

Figure 4. Don't Ask, Don't Tell: 15 Questions That Spell "L-a-w-s-u-i-t"

The following are inappropriate pre-employment inquiries. They should not be asked of, or answered by, former employers during the reference check process.

- How old is this person?

- What is this person's race or nationality?

- Does this individual have any physical or psychological limitations?

- Is this person married, single, widowed, or divorced?

- Does this person have children?

- Is this person "straight" or "gay"?

- On what day of the week does this person attend religious services?

- Has this person ever filed an EEOC charge or a discrimination lawsuit against your company?

- Has this person ever been involved in a union or union organization effort at your company?

- Has this person filed any workers' compensation claims?

- How much leave has this person taken under the Family and Medical Leave Act?

- To your knowledge, has this person ever been arrested?

- Have this person's wages ever been garnished?

- What is this person's native language?

- When did this person become a U.S. citizen?

public, was unable to complete her work on time, and had to meet with a therapist twice a week for three months."

You now have knowledge that Sarah has a psychological disorder. You cannot use this reference information as the basis for rejecting Sarah, because that would amount to disability discrimination in violation of the

Americans with Disabilities Act. Instead, you should apply a second rule for getting nondiscriminatory references: If a reference tells you information about an applicant's legally protected characteristics, do not record, repeat, or rely on this information for the purpose of making employment decisions. If you write down in your notes what the former supervisor said about Sarah's "manic depression" and the applicant is not hired and files a charge of discrimination, how is it going to look to the Equal Employment Opportunity Commission (EEOC) when you produce these notes during the investigation of the charge? Most likely, the EEOC will believe that the "manic depression" played an important part in the hiring decision. If it wasn't important, why was it written down?

Another potential problem can occur in the way unfavorable reference information is used. It would be discriminatory to use a negative reference as a basis for rejecting a minority candidate, but to disregard a similarly bad reference when deciding on a nonminority candidate.

The Fair Credit Reporting Act

Many organizations outsource reference checking and background screening. Those who do so must comply with the Fair Credit Reporting Act (FCRA) and any applicable state credit check laws.

The FCRA is a federal law that establishes several requirements for employers who use "consumer reports" prepared by "consumer reporting agencies" for employment purposes. A consumer report is a written, oral, or other communication that contains information about an individual's credit standing, credit capacity, creditworthiness, character, general reputation, personal characteristics, or mode of living. An "investigative" consumer report is a consumer report about an individual that is obtained by personal interviews with neighbors, friends, and associates. Consumer reporting agencies assemble or evaluate information for the purpose of furnishing consumer reports to third parties.

If an employer uses an outside firm to conduct reference or other background checks, it must follow FCRA disclosure requirements before obtaining a consumer report. It must also comply with the FCRA's adverse action requirements if it decides to reject a job candidate based on information contained in a consumer report. These requirements are described in detail in Chapter 5.

State Laws

Many states have responded to the unfairness and uncertainty of the reference-checking dilemma by enacting laws to clarify rights and responsibilities in this area. Such laws typically address one or more of the following issues: 1) immunity from liability, 2) prohibitions against blacklisting, and 3) service letter requirements. The specific provisions of reference-checking legislation vary from state to state and are beyond the scope of this book; however, employers should be aware of, and comply with, the applicable reference laws in each state in which they have employees.

Immunity

Thirty-five states have passed laws that protect employers by granting them immunity from civil liability for truthful, good-faith references. These immunity provisions provide a safe harbor, in addition to applicable common law defenses, against defamation, invasion of privacy, or other tort lawsuits (see Table 1).

There is considerable variation in reference-checking immunity statutes. Generally, though, state reference-checking immunity statutes

---

Table 1. States with Reference Immunity Laws*

Alaska	Maine	Texas
Arizona	Maryland	Utah
Arkansas	Michigan	Virginia
California	Minnesota	Wisconsin
Colorado	Montana	Wyoming
Delaware	Nevada	
Florida	New Mexico	* as of December 31, 2000;
Georgia	North Dakota	for updates, check the SHRM
Hawaii	Ohio	web site at
Idaho	Oklahoma	http://www.shrm.org
Illinois	Oregon	
Indiana	Rhode Island	
Iowa	South Carolina	
Kansas	South Dakota	
Louisiana	Tennessee	

- apply to references requested by the employee or a prospective employer about current or former employees;
- define the scope of information that may be disclosed in a reference (and typically permit disclosures about job performance); and
- provide conditional rather than absolute immunity from lawsuits.

Often the statutes specify that an employer will be presumed to be acting in good faith (and thus be immune from civil liability) unless the current or former employee can prove that the reference provided was knowingly false, deliberately misleading, malicious, or in violation of civil rights laws.

Blacklisting

Twenty-seven states have laws that prohibit employers from "blacklisting" employees or taking other steps for the purpose of preventing the future employment of these individuals. Table 2 lists states that have enacted anti-blacklisting statutes. These statutes often include penalties, such as fines or even jail time, for violations.

The definition of what constitutes blacklisting varies from state to state, but may include activities such as distributing rosters of blacklisted employees, notifying other employers that a particular employee has been blacklisted, or using threats or force to prevent the employment or obtain the discharge of a specific worker. Some of the blacklisting laws specifically permit employers to provide good-faith job references.

Service Letters

Thirteen states require employers to supply written statements that contain factual information about former employees' service with the employer, either to the employees or to prospective employers. Table 2 lists the states with such service-letter laws.

Employers' service letter obligations vary significantly among the states having such laws. In some states, only certain types of employers (such as public contractors, utilities, or health care organizations) are required to prepare service letters. The required content of such letters differs widely among states. Some of the types of information that may be required by states with service-letter laws include length of service, type of service, qualifications, experience, salary, and reasons for separation. Some service-letter laws require an employee to have a minimum tenure

Table 2. States with Blacklisting or Service-Letter Laws*

Blacklisting Laws		
	Nevada	Indiana
Alabama	New Mexico	Kansas
Arizona	New York	Maine
Arkansas	North Carolina	Minnesota
California	North Dakota	Missouri
Colorado	Oklahoma	Montana
Connecticut	Oregon	Nebraska
Florida	Texas	Nevada
Hawaii	Utah	Ohio
Idaho	Virginia	Oklahoma
Indiana	Washington	Washington
Iowa	Wisconsin	
Kansas		* as of December 31, 2000
Maine	**Service Letter Laws**	
Minnesota	California	
Montana	Delaware	

before an employer is obligated to prepare service letters, or limit the time period in which a service-letter request can be made.

International Laws

In recent years, the number of U.S. companies that operate outside of the United States, or that hire individuals who are employed in other countries, has been increasing. Just as U.S. employers need to comply with the reference-checking laws of the states in which they operate, they also must follow laws of the countries in which they are seeking or responding to reference requests. While a global examination of reference checking is beyond the scope of this book, Appendix B provides a European perspective on legal issues in reference checking.

Employers who will be getting or giving references outside the United States should seek advice and assistance from professionals who are knowledgeable in international employment law and the laws of the particular countries in which the reference-check activities will take place.

CHAPTER 3

Practicalities: Giving References

The Balancing Act

When it comes to giving references, few employers follow the Golden Rule ("do unto others as you would have others do unto you"). While it is standard practice for employers to actively seek in-depth information about applicants from past employers, most employers are tight-lipped when asked to reveal such information about their former and current employees. The fear of lawsuits has led to the prevalence of restrictive policies on giving references.

Responding to reference inquiries requires employers to balance the risk of liability for wrongful disclosures against the desire to provide information that is helpful to other employers and fair to current and former employees. Typically, employers tip the scales toward avoiding litigation, forgoing several benefits that might result from fuller disclosures. However, employers should be aware that they can take many actions to minimize the legal risks of giving references while still providing useful information to other employers.

Out of Balance: Typical Approaches to Giving References

Among the ways employers can choose to respond to reference requests are 1) refuse to provide any information; 2) verify only basic employment information; or 3) provide substantive information about job performance, qualifications, and work-related behaviors.

The "No Comment" Approach

At one extreme, employers may refuse to provide references of any sort. Unfortunately, this "no comment" approach is not uncommon. The

1998 SHRM reference-checking survey reported that 19% of respondents do not give references when asked. This strict method of handling reference inquiries may help insulate organizations from defamation, invasion of privacy, and negligent misrepresentation lawsuits, but it can create other problems for the organization, such as adversely affecting outplacement efforts, unemployment taxes, and employee morale. In addition, when supervisors and human resource professionals are instructed not to divulge reference information, employers may unintentionally create the wrong impression about former employees. Potential employers may assume that no information is being provided because of problems with the individual. Consequently, those responding to reference inquiries in a "no comment" environment need to communicate that adherence to this zero-information policy should not be misinterpreted as an unfavorable reference against the employee in question.

Moreover, human nature being what it is, it will be difficult, if not impossible, to ensure full compliance with a "no comment" policy. A survey by Accountemps revealed that the executives polled made exceptions to a no-reference policy 47% of the time where their experience with the former employee was positive.[11] These practices seemingly harm no one; however, if these practices have an impact on members of protected classes, then valid discrimination claims may arise if favorable references are given to "good" employees and none are given for "bad" employees.

Generally speaking, the "no comment" approach is not part of the solution; it is part of the problem.

The "Name, Rank, and Serial Number" Approach

A majority of employers will share at least some information when contacted for references. The SHRM study revealed that 76% of survey respondents provide references on request. As Table 3 illustrates, the results of the 1998 SHRM survey indicate that, while virtually all employers regularly provide dates of employment and many will comment on salary history and eligibility for rehire, few will comment on work habits, personality traits, interpersonal skills, or bizarre or violent behaviors.

The survey indicates that the predominant method of handling reference requests is to give neutral references limited to confirming basic facts—such as dates of employment and salary history. Many employment attorneys advocate this "name, rank, and serial number" approach

Table 3. Reference Information Regularly Provided when Requested

Information	Percent
Dates of employment	98
Eligibility for rehire	42
Salary history	41
Reason candidate left previous employer	19
Qualification for a particular job	18
Overall impression of employability	16
Work habits (absence, tardiness, etc.)	13
Human relations skills	11
Violent/bizarre behavior	8
Personality traits	7

Source: Extrapolated from 1998 SHRM Reference-Checking Survey

because it minimizes the employer's potential exposure to reference lawsuits, at least if the information provided is accurate.

Although effective in reducing risk, the "name, rank, and serial number" strategy has obvious drawbacks. One is that its popularity has created major barriers to the free flow of information employers need to make sound hiring decisions. As a result, "problem employees" find it easier to hide past misdeeds and strong performers find it difficult to confirm past work accomplishments. Moreover, adherence to neutral reference policies with respect to potentially violent or abusive former employees raises significant ethical concerns.

The "Ad Hoc" Approach

Riskiest of all policies are those that permit supervisors to give or withhold references as they please, without any company-wide standards. Typically, employers who maximize the discretion of supervisors in this manner provide minimal training to these supervisors on how to exercise such discretion in a legal and effective manner.

Achieving Balance: How to Decrease Legal Risks while Providing Substantive References

When considering how to handle reference requests most employers ask, "How can we minimize our exposure to lawsuits when responding to reference inquiries?" A more positive approach is to ask, "How can we give substantive references in ways that will minimize our exposure to lawsuits?"

This latter question is simpler to answer than you may think. A study of reference-checking lawsuits in Washington, Idaho, and Alaska found that employers were held liable only where they had provided false statements about former employees.[12] This study indicates that employers can give useful, in-depth references to potential employers provided they implement safeguards to ensure the references are truthful and job-related.

To establish a framework in which safe and informative responses to reference inquiries can be provided, employers should develop

- a written *policy* on how reference requests will be handled;
- a reference *authorization form* for employee consent and waiver of liability;
- savvy and consistent *procedures* for responding to reference requests; and
- appropriate reference *documentation and record keeping practices* that comply with applicable laws.

Reference Policy

A clear, concise, and complete policy will lay the foundation for litigation-proof references. Surprisingly, given the universal concern about the legal risks in giving references, many employers have never put their reference-checking policies in writing. Often, these are the employers using the ad hoc approach. According to the 1998 SHRM study, 42% of survey respondents did not have written policies on giving references. If a policy isn't written, it is probably not a policy at all, but rather a handy excuse for not doing something.

A written policy is easier for employers to communicate and enforce than are unwritten rules (Figure 5, "Sample Policy on Providing Employment References").

Figure 5. Sample Policy on Providing Employment References

Scope

This is a mandatory policy governing any release of information about current or former employees. Violation of this policy will be considered cause for discipline up to and including termination.

Persons Who May Provide References

References may be provided only by the human resources department or management representatives in the chain of command above the person regarding whom a reference is being requested.

To Whom May References Be Provided

References may be provided only to bona fide prospective employers of current or former employees. Precautions should be taken to ensure that reference requests are legitimate, such as a) requiring the prospective employer to send a letter on company letterhead requesting the reference; b) obtaining the business card of the person requesting the reference; or c) telephoning the person back to verify that he or she is indeed employed by the company.

What Information May Be Provided

Only job-related information may be provided to persons requesting information on current or former employees. Under no circumstances should information be provided regarding the employee's race, religion, national origin, health, childrearing, sexual preference, veteran status, workers' compensation history, complaints about alleged discrimination, political views, or private affairs.

Employee Consent/Release Form

It is the policy of the company not to disclose any information about employees unless and until the company has received an originally signed Employee Consent/Release Form (ECR Form) signed by the employee for whom the reference is requested. A copy of the required form—available from the human resources department—is reproduced below. The ECR Form must be delivered to the human resources department *before* any information is released.

Continued next page

Figure 5 *continued*. Sample Policy on Providing Employment References

Record of References Provided

It is the policy of the company that whenever an employment reference is given, the person giving the reference must complete a Record of Employee Reference Form (REF Form) so the company will have documentation of what information was—and was not—provided to the person requesting the reference. A copy of the required form—available from the human resources department—is reproduced below. The REF Form must be delivered to the human resources department within twenty-four hours of any information being released.

Confidentiality

Except as provided by this policy, all employee information is considered confidential.

Policy Guidance

You are encouraged to contact human resources with any questions about this policy.

At a minimum, the reference policy should cover

- who may provide references;
- to whom references may be provided;
- conditions for releasing information;
- the type of information that may be given; and
- possible disciplinary action for violations of the policy.

The policy should be distributed and discussed with supervisors and employees. Supervisors need to understand the "do's" and "taboos" of providing references and the consequences of failing to follow the policies. Employees should be made aware of the policy so there are no misunderstandings about what topics will or will not be discussed in reference checks. Consequently, this policy should be included in the employee handbook and should be reviewed at termination or whenever an employee is asked to complete a reference authorization form.

Reference Authorization Form

One of the easiest and most effective measures an organization can take to shield itself from liability is to *never* provide any substantive reference information unless the subject of such an inquiry has given his or her prior written authorization to do so. As discussed in Chapter 2, consent is a defense to defamation, invasion of privacy, and other tort claims that can arise from providing improper references.

While you can rely on a written authorization that is provided by the prospective employer (as long as it specifically releases your company and its agents from any liability that may result from providing the reference), it is preferable to develop and use your own form. At a minimum, this reference authorization form should provide unambiguous evidence of the employee's *consent* to references. For even more protection, you can include a *waiver of liability* for any damages resulting from such references. In addition, it should specify what types of information the employee will permit the organization to disclose when contacted for references. A sample form appears in Figure 6, "Sample Employee Consent to Disclose Personnel Information and Release of Liability."

The employee can complete this form at any time before a job reference is given, such as during an exit interview, or as requested by the former employee. The crucial point to remember is that no substantive reference should ever be provided unless and until the individual in question has completed the form.

In situations where the employee has given written authorization, the employer can breathe easy in disclosing substantive, job-related information in response to reference requests. Ironically, even if the employee refuses to sign the authorization form (which would likely occur if the employee wished to hide unfavorable facts about his or her employment), you are still in a position to provide helpful information to prospective employers. How? When the prospective employer calls for a reference, you simply say, "Our company will provide references, including information about a former employee's job performance and qualifications, but only if the individual signs our written consent form. Bob was given the opportunity to complete this form when he left the company, but he chose not to." Although you have not given the prospective employer a substantive reference for Bob, you have truthfully put the company on notice of a possible "red flag" that they should investigate further.

Figure 6. Sample Employee Consent to Disclose Personnel Information
and Release of Liability

Job Reference Policy Statement

Without prior written authorization from former employees, the company
will provide only the following information in response to reference
requests:

1. Hire date and termination date
2. Job titles
3. Earnings

If you desire the company to provide additional information—for example,
evaluation of job performance or reason for termination—then you must
authorize the company to do so and you must release the company from
liability for doing so as provided below.

Employee Consent to Disclose Personnel Information and Release of Liability

I, the undersigned employee, hereby authorize the company to provide
written and verbal information about my employment by the company in
response to any request for such information by a person representing
himself or herself to be checking references in connection with my possible
future employment.

In consideration of the company agreeing to provide such additional
information, I hereby release the company and its officers, directors, agents,
and employees from any and all claims I may have arising out of the
furnishing of such information.

In further consideration of the company agreeing to provide such
additional information, I hereby release any person representing himself
or herself as checking references in connection with my possible future
employment from any and all claims I may have arising out of the
furnishing of such information.

EMPLOYEE

_____   _____
(Signature)   Date

_____
(Print Employee Name)

Termination Practices

A critical variable in the reference liability equation is what is said and done during termination.

For starters, the company's reference policy should be reviewed with all departing employees during the exit interview. Employees should be told that if they use company representatives as references, these individuals will respond to reference requests to the extent allowed by the employer's reference policy and the employee's authorization form. It may also be appropriate to review the employee's personnel file with him or her during the exit process so the employee understands what information will be communicated to prospective employers.

In discharge situations, it is imperative to give the employee the real reasons for termination. These reasons should be based on documented evidence of poor performance or serious misconduct. Failure to do so opens the door for possible compelled self-defamation lawsuits in states where such claims are recognized.

An even bigger legal risk for employers who don't adhere to a "truth in firing" philosophy is the risk of a wrongful discharge lawsuit. A study of almost 1,000 terminated workers in Ohio found that employees who weren't given a reason for their termination were more than ten times more likely to sue their former employer than were employees who were given a reason. More than 20% of the terminated workers studied filed a claim if no reason was given for termination, while less than 2% of the employees who were told why they were being discharged filed a claim.[13]

Regardless of whether termination is voluntary or involuntary, it's inadvisable to provide a "to whom it may concern" recommendation letter for separating employees. Such letters tend to focus on only positive aspects of an employee's performance. Even if all statements in a recommendation letter are accurate, they can mislead by omission and provide the basis for a misrepresentation lawsuit, particularly if the employee exhibited harmful behaviors during employment at your organization.

Even worse would be sending out unsolicited negative letters about former employees to other employers. Such letters may violate state blacklisting laws or provide the basis for a libel lawsuit. Consider the case involving the following letter that singer Diana Ross once wrote about several former employees:

"To Whom It May Concern: The following [seven] people are no longer in my employment: . . . If I let an employee go, it's because either their work or personal habits are not acceptable to me. I do not recommend these people. In fact, if you hear from these people, and they use my name as a reference, I wish to be contacted."[14]

There were a couple of serious problems with this letter that became apparent in the case brought against Ms. Ross by one of these former employees. First, the letter was not solicited by either the recipients or the former employee. Second, it possibly created the erroneous impression that the employee in question had been fired, when in reality the suing employee had quit. The moral of this case: Think before you write any reference letter, and think again if the employee has not asked for such a letter or the letter has not been requested by a prospective employer. Then stop—in the name of libel—before you break the law, and don't write or send such letters.

Handling Reference Inquiries

Reference requests should be handled carefully and consistently. Employers should establish clear guidelines as to who can give references to whom and as to what information can be disclosed. Those providing references should be trained in the proper way to do this.

Who should give references?

The 1998 SHRM reference-checking survey found that 87% of respondent employers delegated primary responsibility for providing references to human resource staff, while supervisors were permitted to give references at only 5% of employers surveyed. The study also found that some employers allowed legal staff, office managers, or representatives from outsourced service companies to disclose reference information.

A key benefit of forwarding reference requests to the human resources department is greater consistency in the nature and content of references provided. In addition, human resources staff is likely to have the necessary expertise and awareness of reference-check liability issues. Moreover, human resources staff will probably have access to current and former employees' personnel files, which makes verification of basic employment data easier.

Centralization of the reference-checking function with the human resources department may be the most desirable approach in theory, but in practice can lead to real problems. Reference checkers routinely bypass the human resources department, and instead contact job applicants' former supervisors directly because they have more direct knowledge of the employees' qualifications and performance and are more likely to talk "off the record." As mentioned previously, even if supervisors are aware of the company's "no comment" or "name, rank, and serial number" policy, many of them will bend the rules and provide substantive references about former employees with whom the supervisor has had a positive experience. A few managers will even break the rules to retaliate against a former "problem employee," relishing the notion that "what goes around comes around."

If your organization delegates exclusive responsibility for handling reference requests to human resources staff, then it should take steps to ensure compliance with this policy, such as taking disciplinary action against individuals who violate the policy. If your organization allows supervisors to give references, training these individuals to handle reference inquiries properly is a must. A simple role-playing exercise is a great way to train reference givers and reference checkers at the same time.

To whom should job references be given?

Provide references only to those parties who have requested them and who have a valid need to know. Giving out information to anyone other than prospective employers who are considering one of your former or current employees for a specific job opening is inviting trouble.

There are some cases where unsuspecting employers have actually provided legally damning references to private investigators hired by former employees. Increasingly, job seekers are turning to "undercover" services available over the Internet that will check on reference givers on the employee's behalf. For fees that typically range from $60-$100, these firms will contact a designated former employer, ask questions about the former employee, and prepare a written report for the former employee. Typically, these services will say that they have been hired by a third party to do a background check for purposes of employment. Although these services don't present themselves as potential employers, they do disguise their identity by using subsidiary companies that operate under varied names for only a few months.

To spot phony reference calls, make sure to ask the caller for information about what the organization does, what job the employee is being considered for, and the caller's position. If an inquiry sounds suspicious, don't provide information until you research the company and verify the caller's position. Better yet, don't give references unless the caller agrees to document the reference request on company letterhead and provide details about the specific position for which the individual is being considered.

What information can be provided?

Employers have a great degree of latitude as to what information they disclose to prospective employers. Nevertheless, former employees can legitimately cry foul when references stray out of bounds because the information provided was false, private, based on unproven gossip, discriminatory, retaliatory, or gratuitous.

To minimize risks of legal liability, any reference information disclosed should satisfy five general tests:

- Legitimate need
- Truth
- Job-relatedness
- Documentation
- Responsiveness.

First, reference information should be provided only to parties who have a legitimate need to know about the former employee. Second, if the information is truthful, it will not provide grounds for a defamation claim. Third, job-related disclosures will not encompass topics that are potentially discriminatory or that create an invasion of privacy. Fourth, if references are based on documented facts, there is evidence to support the accuracy of statements made. Fifth, satisfying the test of responsiveness means that no information will be shared unless it is in response to a specific question.

However, there is an exception to the responsiveness test. It may be advisable to offer facts about a former employee's potential to harm others, even if the person requesting the reference does not raise this issue. In these circumstances, consult an attorney before any disclosures are made.

Typically, reference-checkers may ask about the following topics.

- *Verification of basic facts*
  Dates of employment
  Positions held
  Earnings

- *Employment status*
  Eligibility for rehire
  Reason for leaving
  Overall assessment of employability

- *Performance issues*
  Duties in positions held
  Qualifications for positions held
  Job performance

- *Problems*
  Attendance
  Misconduct
  Violent behavior
  Unusual behavior

- *Other topics*
  Likely situations for the individual to be successful or unsuccessful
  Other individuals familiar with the employee's work

Employers must determine the specific types of information they are willing to provide in response to a legitimate reference inquiry. These topics should be listed on the reference authorization form and should be described in the reference policy.

Consistency in Responding to Reference Inquiries

After an organization determines what types of reference information may be disclosed, this information should be provided consistently for all former or current employees who have given written consent.

When responding in writing to a reference request or completing a reference request form, respond only to those questions that relate to permissible areas of disclosures. Written responses should be returned to the potential employer in an envelope marked *confidential*.

Those who give references over the telephone should be trained to determine if a call is a bona fide request from a prospective employer. If the reference request is legitimate, it's important to stick to the facts. Concrete examples from performance evaluations and other personnel records are factual and helpful to potential employers. Avoid sharing personal opinions, character judgments, or unsubstantiated gossip during reference calls.

It's important to train those individuals who handle reference inquiries to understand the differences between statements that express objective facts and those that are subjective judgments or opinions. For example, it would be improper to say that "Susan is a drug abuser" or "Mark was fired for sexual harassment." But it would be appropriate to comment, if asked about the employee's reason for leaving by a person who has a legitimate, job-related need to know this information, to say: "Susan was terminated after testing positive for controlled substance use during a random drug test" or "As a result of a sexual harassment investigation, the company made the decision to discharge Mark."

Documentation and Record Keeping

In the event a reference ever becomes the basis for legal action by a former employee, it's important to have a paper trail as to how each reference inquiry is handled. An ounce of pretrial documentation will be worth a ton of testimony at trial.

Anyone who receives a request for a telephone reference should note the specifics of the request and the information provided, if any, on a form. See Figure 7, "Sample Record of Employee Reference Form."

Reference documentation should be maintained in the employee's formal personnel records, rather than in a supervisor's "unofficial" employee file. Centralization of reference records in the human resources department ensures that records will remain confidential and be easy to find when needed, and that no "smoking guns" will remain hidden in a supervisor's files only to be discovered too late in the event of litigation or a discrimination charge.

Some organizations not only keep all employee records in the human resources department, but also place *all* of the records for an employee in a single formal personnel file. This may be a convenient record-keeping practice, but it is not legal. Various federal employment statutes require

Figure 7. Sample Record of Employee Reference Form

This form must be completely filled out and delivered to the Human Resources Department within 24 hours of providing any references on current or former employees.

No information about current or former employees may be disclosed unless and until an originally signed Employee Consent/Release Form has been filed with the human resources department.

See Policy No. XX, or consult human resources, for any questions regarding the use of this form.

Record of Employment
Reference for: _____
(Name of Employee)

Date Information Provided: _____

Person Requesting   Name:_____
Information: Title:_____
                           Company:_____
                           Address:_____
                           _____
                           Telephone:_____

Job for Which Employee
Is Being Considered: _____

Form Completed by: _____
Title: _____
Signature: _____

State below any job-related reference information provided or not provided.

Provided	Not Provided	
○	○	Hire/termination date: _____
○	○	Titles: _____
○	○	Compensation: _____
○	○	Reason for leaving: _____
○	○	Evaluation of performance: _____
		_____
○	○	Other: _____

that certain personnel records be kept separately to maintain the confidentiality of sensitive information, protect employee privacy rights, or prevent discrimination.

Employee records should consist of a general personnel file (referred to here as the "employee history file") as well as several other files for specific types of records. The employee history file should include job-related records such as applications, résumés, performance appraisals, disciplinary notices, and status changes. The following categories of information should be kept in separate files.

- Medical records
- EEO data
- I-9s
- Payroll records
- Other confidential information.

Reference documentation should be kept in a separate confidential file rather than in the employee history file. Why? In most cases, references are provided to a prospective employer or obtained from a former employer on the condition that they not be shared with the candidate. Since current employees usually have access to the employee history file, including the information in this file would render assurances of confidentiality to reference-givers meaningless.

While most federal laws do not give employees the right to inspect or copy their personnel files, many states do grant employees access to these files. The states differ as to the nature and extent of access. Typically, state laws limit the right of access to active employees, employees on leaves of absence, or laid-off employees who have reinstatement rights. Although these laws generally allow covered employees to inspect records related to hiring decisions, they do not usually permit employees to review reference documentation.

Retention of Reference Documentation

How long should reference documentation be kept? Various federal, state, and local laws establish minimum record retention periods, but employers may retain personnel records for longer periods at their discretion. Under federal equal employment opportunity laws (for example, Title VII, the Americans with Disabilities Act, and the Age Discrimination in Employment Act), the minimum retention period for personnel records relating to hiring, promotion, demotion, layoffs, and terminations is one year after the record is made or the action is taken, whichever is later, unless the employer is a federal contractor. If a charge or lawsuit is filed, all relevant records must be retained until final disposition.

Thus, except in cases of Equal Employment Opportunity Commission complaints or litigation, reference documentation acquired during the hiring process must be kept for at least one year after it is obtained or the employer hires or rejects the individual; whereas documentation of references given about former employees must be held for one year after the reference is provided. However, Executive Order 11246, the Vocational Rehabilitation Act and the Vietnam Era Veterans' Readjustment Assistance Act establish a two-year minimum for retention of records for some federal contractors. State and local laws may also affect the retention of personnel records, including reference documentation. Some of these laws establish longer minimum retention periods than required under federal law. In such cases, the employer must retain the records for the longer period.

23 Tips for Giving References

The following "tip list" may help keep reference-givers on the right track.

1. Understand that the organizational benefits of providing substantive references include

   Supporting the company's outplacement program;
   Lowering unemployment costs; and
   Rewarding strong performers.

2. Develop a formal policy on handling reference requests. This policy should address

   The type of information that can be disclosed;
   Who is permitted to provide references; and
   The required form of the reference request.

3. Communicate the organization's reference policy to managers and employees and enforce it.

4. Ask separating employees to sign an authorization form permitting the employer to give references to prospective employers. If the employee refuses to sign the form, explain that fact to prospective employers and suggest they discuss this with the candidate.

5. To avoid defamation claims based on compelled self-publication and lawsuits for wrongful discharge, make sure terminated employees are given an accurate reason for the termination, based on documented evidence.

6. Don't provide references for former employees unless you have a written authorization and waiver of liability (either one you've obtained or one provided to you by the prospective employer).

7. Don't provide blank "to whom it may concern" reference letters.

8. When responding to written reference requests, return them to the requester in an envelope marked *confidential*.

9. To maintain consistency and accountability, clearly designate who in the organization has the responsibility and authority to provide reference information.

10. Ask any party requesting a reference if he or she

    Represents a prospective employer of the individual whose reference has been requested and has the former employee's permission to contact the employer.

11. When in doubt about the identity and motives of the person making a telephone inquiry, call the prospective employer to verify the inquirer's position.

12. Communicate only with parties who have a legitimate need for a reference about a former employee. Do not answer reference inquiries made by firms or investigators retained by the former employee or by acquaintances of the former employee.

13. Before giving references on the telephone, ask if the other party is alone and if the conversation is being recorded.

14. Provide only truthful, job-related information when providing references.

15. Use specific examples and facts to provide informative, concrete answers to reference checkers' questions.

16. Ideally, factual information given in references should be based on documentation.

17. Don't volunteer information that is not requested by reference checkers.

18. Don't provide misleading information to reference checkers.

19. Provide the same type of reference information about former employees, at all levels, to the extent the employee has consented to disclosures.

20. Consult an attorney if a reference request pertains to a former employee who exhibited dangerous tendencies.

21. Document the specific responses given to all reference requests on a standardized form.

22. Keep reference documentation confidential.

23. Retain reference records for at least the minimum period required by law.

CHAPTER 4

Practicalities: Getting References Yourself

Hide and Seek

Checking references can be like playing the human resources version of hide and seek. The game usually works this way: The prospective employer, who wants to select the most qualified candidate and avoid liability for negligent hiring, is the seeker of basic factual information and perspectives on applicants' past job performances. Former employers, whose primary objective is typically to avoid defamation, invasion of privacy, and other tort lawsuits, often hide many of these facts by politely, but firmly, saying either nothing about their former employees or providing only "name, rank, and serial number" references in response to the seeker's reference inquiries.

When the reference-checking game is played this way, the good guys lose. Employers lose because without complete information about an applicant's work history, they may make poor hiring decisions, which in turn can lead to absenteeism, discipline problems, high turnover, theft, and unsafe behaviors. Capable and honest workers lose because they cannot provide verbal or written proof of their professional accomplishments. Former employers can also be put at risk for failing to candidly disclose genuine problems with a former employee's performance or conduct. Too often, the only winner in the reference hide-and-seek game is the dishonest applicant who successfully conceals aggressive actions, bizarre behavior, or poor performance from the prospective employer.

Is it possible to change the rules and outcomes in the reference-checking game? You bet! According to the 1998 SHRM reference-checking survey, approximately 15% of surveyed employers prefer to play the game by proxy, obtaining references through an outside agency. For the remaining 85%, the keys to obtaining accurate and useful information from past employers are to

■ Establish *requirements* for pre-employment screening activities;
■ Develop a *written policy* on obtaining references;
■ Collect reference *documentation*;
■ *Involve applicants* actively in the process; and
■ *Communicate skillfully* with reference sources.

Ask Me No Secrets and I'll Tell You No Lies

Falsification of information is rampant in the hiring process. Surveys reveal that from 25% to 40% of applicants lie about, embellish, or conceal their qualifications or backgrounds on résumés or job applications.

Employers have learned to be on the alert for these fabrications. According to the 1998 SHRM reference-checking survey, most employers have discovered falsified information during reference checks (Table 4).

Table 4. Falsified Information Found during Reference Checks

Information Verified	% of Employers Who Found Falsified Information
Length of employment	90
Past salaries	90
Former titles	88
Former employers	84
Criminal records	83
Degrees conferred	78
Schools attended	77
Driving records	76
Credit checks	69
Social Security number	59

Source: Extrapolated from SHRM 1998 Reference-Checking Survey

Employers should keep a few things in mind when they uncover false-hoods or misleading information during the hiring process. First, if a candidate has lied on one area of his or her résumé or application, it's likely he or she lied about other things, too. Second, if a candidate is willing to twist the truth to get a job, he or she may also be dishonest on the job. A study by Checkpoint Systems Inc. of 20,000 randomly selected job applicants revealed that 22.6% could be categorized as a high risk for committing dishonest acts on the job. The study also found that 28.7% of the respondents might be tempted to steal from their employer, and that 8.3% had actually stolen money in the past three years.[15]

These disheartening statistics underscore the importance of thorough pre-employment screening processes, designed to uncover the hidden truths about job applicants and weed out undesirable individuals before they wreak havoc in your workplace.

Ground Rules for Pre-employment Screening

To succeed in the hiring hide-and-seek game, employers should establish appropriate requirements for pre-employment screening. These policies should focus on practices that increase the likelihood of the organization hiring the best-qualified candidates and avoiding negligent hiring claims.

Minimum Requirements

At a minimum, three steps should be taken before hiring an individual for any job:

1. **Verify employment history for the past five to seven years.** Due diligence in hiring begins with confirmation of job candidates' work histories. Fortunately, most employers seek this information. According to the 1998 SHRM reference-checking study, 81% of employers regularly verify former employers and 79% confirm dates of employment.

   Gaps in an applicant's stated employment history are tip-offs to possible problems. Where there are such discrepancies, the applicant may be camouflaging a discharge, job-hopping, or imprisonment.

2. **Verify educational credentials and licenses required for the position.** Some of the most common applicant falsehoods concern educational attainments. Applicants may list phony degrees from colleges they

never attended. Or they may stretch the truth by claiming a degree from a school they attended, but never graduated from.

Usually, employers can verify degrees by contacting the educational institution that issued the degree. Many schools will provide this verification over the phone, but others may require a release from the applicant, or only give verifications by mail. Academic transcripts are typically available for a small fee and a written release from the individual whose transcript has been requested.

Professional licenses can be verified through the appropriate state licensing authorities. Such checks should include the current status and expiration date of the individual's license.

3. **Check references.** How many references should be checked? One is never enough. Two references may be minimally sufficient, if they provide similar views of the candidate. Optimally, at least three references should be obtained, especially for high-level or sensitive positions involving access to valuable property or unsupervised contact with persons needing special care. Additional reference checks may be necessary if references provide contradictory views of the candidate.

Consistent with these guidelines, organizations responding to the 1998 SHRM survey reported checking an average of 2.7 references.

An effective reference check will go beyond mere verification of basic facts about dates of employment, positions held, and earnings. It should include questions relating to the applicant's performance, qualifications, reason for leaving, problem behaviors, and suitability for the new position. The tips and techniques described in this chapter will help employers unearth information in these areas. However, even if attempts to get substantive references are sometimes unsuccessful, such efforts provide proof that an employer was reasonable, and not negligent, in its hiring practices.

When to Do More

Employers may decide to go beyond these minimally reasonable inquiries of applicants' backgrounds for all new hires. If this is not possible, employers should instead conduct more extensive background investigations for high-risk jobs where the employee will have the ability to cause serious harm. Positions that entail substantial risk include those where the employee will

- be in contact with vulnerable individuals (such as children, the elderly, patients, or the disabled);
- have access to dwellings;
- operate vehicles;
- handle money and other valuables;
- have access to weapons, drugs, or dangerous substances;
- have extensive or unsupervised public contact; or
- supervise others.

What Additional Investigation Is Necessary

When filling such high-risk positions, employers should take extra precautions during the hiring process to identify and reject unsuitable individuals. A variety of investigations can be undertaken to check applicants' backgrounds. Four of the most commonly used methods are as follows.

Criminal Records Check

A surprisingly high percentage of applicants have a history of criminal behavior. According to Avert, Inc., one of ten applicants had a criminal record in the past seven years. Clearly, the prevalence of applicants who have engaged in criminal activity and the tendency of some of these individuals to withhold conviction information deliberately from potential employers underscore the prudence of conducting criminal background checks, especially for jobs where an employee is in a position of trust.

Checking criminal history is easier said than done, but many employers make the effort nevertheless. According to a survey conducted in 2000 by *Human Resource Executive* magazine and ERC Dataplus, 80% of the organizations polled perform checks for criminal convictions.[16] While some organizations require criminal background checks for all employees, others conduct background checks only for selected positions.

Employers who want to check an applicant's criminal history must navigate a maze of court records because no national database of criminal records is available to employers or the public. The National Crime

Information Center keeps records on most felonies and some misde-meanors, but access to this national information is restricted to law enforcement agencies and some employers (including airlines and finan-cial institutions).

Most states have central repositories of criminal records from state police and state courts. Some states allow access to these records for pre-employment screening purposes. However, many of these states have severely restrictive requirements for obtaining statewide criminal infor-mation—such as extensive documentation or fingerprints. Information obtained from state repositories may not be current or accurate.

The county courthouse, where felony records are maintained, is the repository of the most thorough and up-to-date information. It is stan-dard to search records in the county where the applicant lives, as well as neighboring counties, especially if a large city is nearby. Records should also be checked in counties where the applicant has worked, as well as counties of prior residence if the applicant has moved frequently.

Credit Report

Credit checks can provide information about an individual's credit stand-ing, creditworthiness, and credit capacity and give details about credit limits, current balances, payment history, bankruptcies, and tax liens. According to the *Human Resource Executive*/ERC Dataplus 2000 back-ground-checking survey, 34% of employers surveyed perform credit checks.

Credit reports are frequently done on candidates applying for positions that involve financial responsibility. The report helps employers ascertain whether the potential employee's financial status might present a risk in a position involving handling money or exercising financial discretion. The Fair Credit Reporting Act regulates the gathering and use of credit infor-mation furnished to employers by consumer reporting agencies. The requirements of this federal law are discussed in Chapter 5. Many states have also enacted laws restricting access to and use of credit histories.

If a credit report reveals that an applicant has declared bankruptcy, been insolvent before filing bankruptcy, or not paid a debt that has been discharged in bankruptcy, it is illegal under the U.S. Bankruptcy Code for an employer to discriminate against the applicant on that basis.

Motor Vehicle Record

It is critical to check the driving record of any individual who will operate a company vehicle at any time, or who will drive personal or rental vehicles on company business. One-half of the employers responding to the *Human Resource Executive*/ERC Dataplus 2000 background check survey checked motor vehicle records.

Unfortunately, it is all too common for individuals with terrible driving records to apply for, and get, jobs requiring them to operate trucks or cars. Avert, Inc., reports that two of five applicants whose driving history is screened had at least one moving violation on their driving records.

If an employer fails to investigate driving history, an individual who has a record of drunk or reckless driving may end up behind the wheel. Motor vehicle records (MVRs) are available from state motor vehicle departments rather than nationally. Usually an MVR covers at least three years of driving history. It will typically list license status, license class, expiration date, traffic violations, arrests and convictions for driving under the influence, and license suspensions or cancellations.

If an applicant's license is not from his or her state of residence (or recent residence), this may be a tip-off that the individual lost his or her license in that state.

Social Security Number Verification

If a credit report is obtained, an applicant's Social Security number (SSN) will automatically be verified; however, there are reasons to verify an applicant's SSN even when a credit check is unnecessary. For example, applicants sometimes provide an incorrect SSN. Avert, Inc., reports that 6% of their SSN inspections revealed an invalid SSN. Other applicants may provide the correct number, but falsify prior addresses.

An SSN check will confirm the applicant's name and SSN. Employers may also use this type of check to obtain up to ten prior addresses for the applicant. SSN checks will also provide the names of anyone who has used a particular number. Although they can be a useful tool for background checks, SSN verifications are not conducted on a widespread basis. Only 22% of organizations polled in the *Human Resource Executive*/ERC Dataplus 2000 background check survey performed SSN checks.

There is no "one-size-fits-all" approach to background investigations; rather, which investigation tools are appropriate depends on the nature of the job. For instance, it would be prudent to check the motor vehicle records of applicants for truck driver positions and to run a credit report on bank teller applicants. In most situations, though, it would be wasteful or even risky to procure a credit report on truck driver applicants or to check the driving record of bank teller applicants. Since these checks would not be job-related, any adverse impact on a protected class could result in a discrimination claim or could be alleged to be a pretext for discrimination.

Specific pre-employment screening techniques should not be used if they tend to have an adverse impact on members of protected classes, unless these practices are job-related and necessary for the employer's business. For example, credit checks tend to have an adverse impact on women and minorities. Consequently, they should not be conducted unless there is a business justification to do so, such as for positions requiring the individual to handle money or other valuables. Similarly, information about arrests, as opposed to convictions, should not be sought or used as the basis for making hiring decisions. In fact, some state laws prohibit employers from using arrest records in making employment decisions or seeking information about arrests from the applicant or any other source.

Employers need to weigh the nature and extent of risks of potential injury that could result by hiring an unfit individual for a particular position against the costs and time required to conduct particular types of investigations. Employers also need to decide whether to handle background inquiries and reference checks internally or outsource them to investigation firms or third-party vendors. Chapter 5 provides pointers on how to select and use outside professionals for these activities.

It's My Policy and I'm Sticking to It

Just as employers should have a written policy on giving references, they also should have a policy on getting references. Any such policy should require that all applicants sign an authorization form in which they consent to any necessary reference or background checks and release the organization and third parties from any liability for conducting these activities (Figure 8, "Sample General Policy on Checking References for All New Hires"). An applicant's refusal to sign this form should be grounds for rejection.

The reference check policy should also address how many references will be sought, from whom, and by whom. It should also specify the types of background information the employer may obtain about the applicant.

It makes sense to adopt a requirement that *no* individual will be hired unless and until satisfactory references are first obtained. This may seem like an overly strict policy given sometimes stiff competition for even minimally qualified employees and the need for speed in hiring. However, to hire someone without the benefit of adequate job references is to risk employing an unfit individual whose poor performance or dangerous propensities could expose your company to theft, accidents, workplace violence, or a negligent hiring lawsuit.

Figure 8. Sample General Policy on Checking References for All New Hires

Scope

This is a mandatory policy applicable to the hiring of any new employee.

Mandatory Reference Checks

Appropriate reference checks must be conducted for each prospective new hire. At least one satisfactory reference not provided by the applicant must be obtained *before* any job offer is extended by the company. Any employment offer thereafter extended by the company is contingent on the company receiving such additional, satisfactory references on the candidate as are deemed appropriate for the position in question or the particular circumstances. Separate policies have been established for checking references for certain sensitive positions, including all management and supervisory positions. The human resources department and persons responsible for hiring may request additional references as may be warranted under the particular circumstances.

Persons Who May Check References

References may be requested only by the human resources department, the person responsible for hiring for the position in question, or under the

Continued next page

Figure 8 *continued.* Sample General Policy on Checking References for
All New Hires

close and confidential supervision of the person responsible for hiring for
the position in question.

Method of Checking References

References may be checked either verbally or in writing. Under no circumstances may references be checked unless and until the company has
received an originally signed Applicant Consent/Release Form (ACR Form)
signed by the job applicant. A copy of the required form—available from
the human resources department—is reproduced below. The ACR Form
must be delivered to the human resources department *before* any references are checked.

What Information May Be Requested

Only job-related information may be checked pertaining to applicants for
employment. Under no circumstances should information be requested
regarding the applicant's race, religion, national origin, health, plans for having children, sexual preference, veteran status, workers' compensation history, complaints about alleged discrimination, political views, or private affairs.

Record of References Obtained

It is the policy of the company that whenever an employment reference is
checked, the person checking the reference must complete an Applicant
Reference-Checking Form (ARC Form) so that the company will have documentation of its reference-checking process. A copy of the required form—
available from the human resource department—is reproduced below.
Completed ARC Forms should be delivered to the human resource department within one week of a new hire's start date.

Confidentiality

Except as provided by this policy, all employee information is considered
confidential.

Policy Guidance

You are encouraged to contact human resources with any questions about
this policy.

To hasten pre-employment screening, some employers use a fast-track process of extending job offers, or even allow an employee to begin work, before references have been checked. In these situations, the offer or continued employment is conditioned on the receipt of acceptable references. This fast-track process can easily derail when negative references surface after a candidate has changed jobs, relocated, or even started work. The employer is then placed in the awkward position of rescinding a job offer or firing a brand-new—but unsuitable—employee, and usually the affected individual will demand to know why. Whether or not a full explanation is given, the individual is likely to believe an injustice has occurred and may take legal action against the employer and parties who gave negative references. In such a situation, a signed reference authorization form will probably protect the reference giver, but probably will not protect the employer who hired the employee before references were checked.

Put It in Writing

A written reference check policy lays the foundation for a successful reference check program. Strengthen this program with thorough documentation. An updated employment application form, a release signed by the applicant, and a standardized reference response form will provide solid proof of due diligence in the event of a lawsuit for negligent hiring.

Employment Application

Application forms should provide candidates with conspicuous notice of your reference-checking practices. Include a statement on the application that your company may make inquiries into the candidate's professional and personal background during the selection process. If your organization will not hire individuals unless it receives favorable references, the application should disclose this practice.

The application should also state that giving false information during the hiring process is grounds for rejection or immediate termination. Such a strong declaration of company policy is itself a deterrent to would-be perpetrators of hiring fraud. In addition, the application form must contain a signature and date line. Employers should insist that the form be signed and should not consider applicants who have not signed the application.

Applications should be used to solicit basic information for reference checks. Require applicants to provide all names and nicknames used. Most applications require candidates to provide employment history and relevant details; in addition, applications should require a separate section for listing and explaining periods of unemployment. The application should also require the applicant to provide his or her SSN and driver's license number (if the position requires operation of a vehicle on company business).

To encourage complete answers, the application form should contain ample space for responses and indicate that additional sheets should be used if necessary.

Completed applications should be scrutinized carefully for red flags such as

- blanks (especially with respect to reasons for leaving jobs);
- gaps in employment;
- periods of employment that do not match those listed on the résumé;
- periods of employment as a "consultant" (this may be a smoke screen for periods of unemployment, so it is important to verify that the individual worked consistently during these periods);
- lack of detail or instructions to "see résumé";
- illegible writing (scribbles may mean that the applicant is attempting to conceal unfavorable information); or
- no signature.

If an applicant is considered for hire in spite of these red flags, the problems indicated need to be covered thoroughly in the interview and investigated carefully in reference or background checks.

Applicant Authorization

Just as an employer should never give references without the employee's consent, it should never get references or conduct other background investigations without the applicant's prior knowledge and written approval (Figure 9, "Sample Applicant's Consent to Obtain Background Information and Release of Liability"). This documentation is powerful insurance against reference-related litigation and it can be provided to reluctant reference sources to encourage more candid responses.

The applicant consent form should authorize the company to contact professional and personal references of the employer's own choosing and

Figure 9. Sample Applicant's Consent to Obtain Background Information and Release of Liability

Job Reference Policy Statement

It is the policy of the company to conduct such reference checks and background investigations as are deemed appropriate on all applicants for employment. No applicant will be hired unless and until the company receives such background information as it, in its sole discretion, deems satisfactory to make any hiring decision.

To assist the company in obtaining the references and other background information necessary to consider applications for employment, it is the policy of the company that all applicants must complete the following Consent to Obtain Background Information Form.

Consent to Obtain Background Information

I, the undersigned applicant, hereby authorize the company to obtain and verify verbally or in writing such information about my background and qualifications for employment as the company, in its sole discretion, deems relevant to its decision whether to hire me for the position I am applying for, including without limitation professional and personal references, employment verifications, educational verifications, license and credentials verifications, criminal records, motor vehicle records, credit reports, and Social Security number verifications.

In consideration of the company considering my application for employment, I hereby release the company and its officers, directors, agents, and employees from any and all claims I may have arising out of the obtaining and verification of such information.

I hereby authorize any and all persons to disclose information to the company about my previous employment or suitability for future employment.

In consideration of any person agreeing to provide information to the company as authorized by this form, I hereby release any such person and any affiliated officers, directors, agents, and employees from any and all claims I may have arising out of the disclosure of such information.

APPLICANT

_____   _____

(Signature)   Date

_____

(Print Applicant Name)

to conduct other necessary investigations to determine the applicant's suitability. It is recommended that the form include a complete waiver of liability for any claims the applicant may have against the prospective employer and any organization or individual providing reference or background information.

Reference-Checking Form

To promote consistency and save time in reference checks, develop a standard form to document reference contacts and their outcomes. All reference inquiries—even those in which the contact refuses to provide any information—should be documented using these forms. Even unsuccessful reference checks demonstrate an employer's attempt to reasonably investigate a candidate's background and avoid negligent hiring decisions.

This form should contain space to record information about

- the individual contact (date and time of contact, method of contact, name, address, telephone number, and title of person contacted, relationship to applicant, etc.);
- verification of basic facts and employment history (period of employment, earnings, positions held, job responsibilities, eligibility for rehire, etc.);
- assessment of the candidate's ability to perform the job in question (past work performance, job-related strengths and weaknesses, areas for development, unusual incidents or behavior, etc.); and
- the names of other people to contact about the applicant's work and professional background.

See Figure 10, "Sample Reference-Checking Form."

Figure 10. Sample Reference-Checking Form

Applicant: _____

Reference: _____

Job Sought: _____

Employer: _____

Title: _____

Address: _____

Checked by: _____

Title: _____

Telephone: _____

Date/Time: _____

Relationship to Applicant: _____

Contact Method: _____

Basic Facts

1. When did _____ start working for your company?

   _____

2. What was _____'s last day working for your company?

   _____

3. What was _____'s position?

   _____

4. How was _____ paid by your company—salary, hourly, commission?

   _____

5. What was the gross pay of _____ the last month/year of employment?

   _____

6. Did that include overtime, bonuses, or incentive pay?

   _____

Continued next page

Figure 10 *continued*. Sample Reference-Checking Form

Employment History

1. What were _____'s duties?
    _____
    _____
    _____

2. From your perspective, what is the most challenging aspect of that job?
    _____
    _____
    _____

3. How many other employees hold the same position?
    _____

4. How large is your company?
    _____

5. How large is the department _____ worked in?
    _____

6. Was there anything unique about your company or _____'s job that you think would be important for a potential employer of _____ to know?
    _____
    _____
    _____

7. Are there any particular customers or clients _____ worked with closely and regularly?
    _____
    _____

8. Who else at your company would be familiar with _____'s job performance?
    _____
    _____

Continued next page

Employability

1. What would you say were _____'s strengths in this position?

   _____

   _____

   _____

2. What would you say were _____'s areas of weakness in this position?

   _____

   _____

   _____

3. How did _____'s performance compare to the performance of the person now/previously performing the job?

   _____

   _____

   _____

4. What would you say is _____'s most significant accomplishment with your company?

   _____

   _____

   _____

5. On a scale of 1 to 10 (with 10 being the best performance possible), how would you rate the overall quality of _____'s job performance?

   _____

6. Did you find _____ to be a dependable employee?

   _____

7. Approximately how often was _____ absent/tardy?

   _____

8. Did you find _____ to be a person of high integrity?

   _____

9. Was _____ well-liked by coworkers?

   _____

Continued next page

Figure 10 *continued*. Sample Reference-Checking Form

10. How would you describe _____ in terms of professionalism?
    _____
    _____

11. What characteristics do you find the most admirable in _____?
    _____
    _____

12. What characteristics do you find the least admirable in _____?
    _____
    _____

13. What changes, if any, have you observed in _____ during the time you worked together?
    _____
    _____

14. Would you recommend _____ for a position as a _____?
    If not, why not?
    _____
    _____
    _____

15. What is your assessment as to how well-suited _____ is to a career in _____?
    _____
    _____
    _____

Problems

1. Why did _____ leave your company?
    _____
    _____
    _____
    _____

Continued next page

2. Would _____ be eligible for rehire by your company? If not, is that because of a general policy or something about _____ in particular?

_____

_____

_____

3. Are you aware of any problems with _____'s job performance? If so, how were the problems addressed?

_____

_____

_____

4. To your knowledge, was _____ ever investigated or disciplined for serious misconduct such as violence, theft, drug or alcohol use, sexual harassment, or violations of company policy? If so, what where the alleged circumstances and what was the outcome?

_____

_____

_____

_____

_____

5. To your knowledge, did _____ ever engage in any unsafe or violent behavior on the job? If so, how were the problems addressed?

_____

_____

_____

_____

_____

CHECKER'S COMMENTS:

_____

_____

_____

_____

_____

_____

_____

_____

_____

I Get By with a Little Help from My Applicants

One mistake many employers make in their reference-checking practices is to unnecessarily shoulder the entire burden of obtaining reference information. Much of the burden can, and should, be shifted to the applicant before, during, and after the interview. After all, the applicant is the one seeking employment with your organization. The applicant should not be treated like an innocent bystander while you struggle valiantly to get a complete picture of his or her work history from former employers. To expedite the process and increase the usefulness of information obtained, enlist the applicant to help your organization with reference checks.

Application Process

There are several duties you can assign applicants to do during the initial application process to help you get ready to conduct pre-employment screening activities.

First, require the applicant to complete the application and the reference check authorization form on-site. This will ensure that the application is not completed by a proxy and will enable the detection of literacy problems.

Second, before the applicant is allowed to submit the application, provide him or her with a written notice that states that the company intends to check the accuracy of the information on the application and résumé and that candidates who provide inaccurate information will be rejected (Figure 11, "Sample Notice to Job Applicants"). Allow the applicant extra time after reading this notice to review the application again for completeness and accuracy. Many applicants will take advantage of this last chance to make corrections before it is too late.

After the application is turned in, inform the applicant that if an interview is scheduled, he or she will need to bring a check stub from the current or last job and a business card (if the applicant has one) to the interview. The check stub can be used to verify current compensation, while the business card will confirm the applicant's current title. If the position requires any licenses or degrees, copies of these should be requested as well. Any mismatches between these documents and what is listed on the application and résumé are obvious warning signs.

Figure 11. Sample Notice to Job Applicants

Verification of Information on Application Materials

It is the policy of the company to verify the accuracy of information provided by applicants on employment applications, résumés, and other application materials through such reference checks, background investigations, and other means as the company, in its sole discretion, deems appropriate.

Documents Required at Time of Interview

All applicants for employment who are selected for an interview are required to provide the following documents at the time of the interview:
1. the most recent check stub from applicant's current or most recent employer;
2. a business card from applicant's current or most recent employer (if employer provided business cards for applicant); and
3. photocopies of any degrees, professional licenses, or certificates obtained by applicant.
Photocopies of these documents will be made and retained as part of your application for employment.

Documents Required upon Hiring

If hired, you will also be required to provide, within three days of your employment, proof of your identity and authorization to work as required by the Immigration Reform and Control Act of 1986. Documents that may be used to establish your identity and authorization to work are listed on the attached Form I-9 required by the U.S. Immigration and Naturalization Service.

Interview Practices

Interviews provide an excellent opportunity for employers to prepare for reference checking. Since most applicants' reference lists include only those people who will speak very highly of them, interviewers should identify the names of several individuals who worked closely with the candidate but were not named on the candidate's own reference list. These names should include the candidate's direct and second-tier supervisors, peers, subordinates, and, if applicable, clients or customers.

Although generally less useful, interviewers may wish to obtain the names of personal references (for example, teachers, local business people, and others acquainted with the applicant outside of the work setting), particularly if the applicant has limited work experience or is returning to the workforce after an extended absence. A comprehensive list of potential references will make it possible for reference checkers to contact a variety of reference sources that have not been preselected by the applicant. It is entirely proper—and recommended—to check references of individuals who are not listed on the applicant's reference list, as long as the applicant is notified on the application and reference authorization form and has given his or her written consent.

To develop this expanded list of references during the interview, you should follow up on the applicant's responses to questions about prior professional experiences, with pointed, specific questions such as the following.

- *What was the name of the individual you worked most closely with on the project you just mentioned?*
- *Who reported to you directly when you managed this group?*
- *Who in the corporate hierarchy, above your immediate supervisor, was aware of the accomplishments you've just described?*

Remind applicants during the interview that your organization will check references before extending an offer. Ask the applicant, "If we contact your last three supervisors, what would they say about you?" The response to this question may alert you to trouble spots, and will also give you the opportunity to assess the congruency of applicants' perceptions of their performance vis-à-vis others' perceptions.

You should also ask if there is someone who should not be contacted for a reference, and why. While it is understandable that an applicant may not want his or her current supervisor contacted (since it may jeopardize his or her job security or working relationship with a boss), it is a definite warning sign if the candidate requests that individuals, other than those at his or her current organization, not be contacted. In either case, the interviewer should ask the applicant why certain individuals should not be contacted. The applicant's answer to this question may be illuminating. For example, if the applicant cites a "personality conflict," "workplace dispute," or a similar reason for not contacting a former or current supervisor, the response could indicate real problems that should be explored in-depth during the interview. To do so, the interviewer can ask the applicant to "tell me more about this situation" and dig deeper with probing follow-up questions.

When an applicant refuses to allow contact with a particular supervisor, a few things can be done to reach a temporary compromise during a reference stalemate. Interviewers can ask for copies of performance appraisals that cover the period of employment in question. The applicant can also provide the names of permissible contacts (for example, other supervisors, clients, or peers) who are familiar with his or her work during this time. Even if the applicant provides appraisals and other reference sources, the employer should consider not hiring the applicant unless the applicant permits contacting the forbidden reference as the final hurdle before an offer is extended.

During the interview, it is also helpful to determine whether the applicant is acquainted with any of your organization's employees. These individuals are likely to be a source of candid information because they place their own judgment and credibility on the line when providing information about an applicant with whom they are acquainted.

Help with Obtaining References

References can be obtained more easily and quickly if the applicant does some of the time-consuming legwork for you. There are several ways in which applicants can assist in the reference-checking process.

First, ask the applicant to make the necessary arrangements for you to talk with the sources you choose. This not only saves time, it also assures the reference sources that they will be providing information at the specific request of the applicant. Second, have the applicant send a copy of his or her résumé to those individuals with whom you wish to speak; this way, you can confirm that the information on the résumé is accurate. Third, request that applicants provide copies of past performance reviews or work samples.

The candidate's efforts in these areas will help you not only to complete reference checks more easily and quickly, but also to gauge how cooperative, resourceful, and diligent the applicant, if hired, may be in helping your organization achieve its other objectives.

Calling All References

Telephone contacts have become employers' method of choice for reference checking; however, references can also be obtained by contacting the references by letter, fax, or e-mail.

In a 1995 SHRM survey, 45% of employers surveyed said they felt comfortable providing information about a candidate's work habits during a telephone conversation, while fewer than one-third (30%) felt comfortable discussing work habits in writing, and only 15% and 9%, respectively, felt comfortable reporting this information via e-mail or fax. The 1998 SHRM reference-checking survey found that 85% of respondents regularly use the telephone to obtain references. These findings probably reflect the time and logistical difficulties of making face-to-face contacts, the lower response rates to written inquiries, and the confidentiality issues that can arise with fax or e-mail (Table 5).

Table 5. Reference-Checking Methods Compared

Method	Time Needed to Initiate/ Conduct Check	Ease of Contacting Reference Source	Likelihood of Obtaining In-Depth Information	Ability to Keep Information Disclosed Confidential
Telephone	10-30 minutes	Varies considerably	Moderate to High	Excellent
Written Request	Less than 10 minutes	Easy	Low	Good
Face-to-Face Contact	Varies considerably	Varies considerably	High	Excellent
Fax	Less than 10 minutes	Easy	Low	Poor
E-mail	Less than 10 minutes	Easy	Low to Moderate	Poor to Fair

Survey findings indicate that in-person reference checks have the added benefit of eliciting the most candid disclosures and allowing the reference checker to observe nonverbal behaviors such as raised eyebrows, closed defensive postures, and lack of eye contact. Consequently, although it usually involves considerable extra effort to have a face-to-face discussion with a reference, such efforts may be worthwhile for key, high-level positions. When in-person reference checking can be accomplished informally via networking contacts, it can be one of the most effective ways to get full and open disclosures about applicants.

Consider the following suggestions to streamline your reference-checking practices and increase your ability to go beyond verifying basic factual information to gathering assessments of candidates' abilities and potential problem areas.

Timing

A survey of *Fortune 500* companies several years ago revealed that about 10% of total time spent on interviewing and hiring was devoted to reference checking.[17] Almost 40% of employers polled in the 1998 SHRM reference-checking survey indicated that they had spent more time reference checking in the past three years. To save time and increase efficiency, reference checks should be saved for the last step in the screening process.

Who Should Contact References

Typically, the responsibility for making reference calls is delegated to one or just a few people in the human resources department. Such centralization of responsibility helps to ensure consistency and expertise in reference checks. Another fairly common approach is for reference checks to be conducted by the person for whom the candidate would work. The advantage of this approach is that an applicant's former supervisors are typically more willing to open up to another supervisor than to human resources staff. Possible drawbacks include a lack of uniformity and skill in obtaining references. Whoever conducts reference checks should be trained in techniques for obtaining in-depth references.

Whom to Contact

There are a few realities to keep in mind when deciding whom to call for references.

First, human resources professionals typically have easy access to former employees' personnel records, so they tend to provide the most accurate verification of basic factual data, including dates of employment, titles, and salary. However, they usually lack first-hand knowledge of employees' job performance and are the least able and willing to share substantive reference information.

Second, former supervisors will have the best knowledge of an applicant's work habits, qualifications, character, suitability for particular jobs, and reasons for leaving. In addition, they tend to be much more likely than human resources representatives to stray from their employers' "name, rank, and serial number" or "no comment" policy, particularly for good former employees.

Third, coworkers, customers, or clients can serve as an alternative or supplementary source of useful information about an applicant's job performance and work behaviors. Generally, these individuals are not restricted by the employer's reference policy, and as a result are usually willing to respond fully to reference inquiries to the extent they have personal knowledge about the applicant.

Fourth, experienced reference checkers have found that, the higher the level of the person contacted, the more likely the person is to provide candid, in-depth assessments of former workers.

These realities suggest that the best initial reference contacts are the individuals who have first-hand information about the applicant—those supervisors, peers, subordinates, clients, and customers mentioned during the interview. Don't go through the human resources department to check references unless supervisors are unable to verify basic factual information. Or, contact human resources as a last resort when a former supervisor has left the company and his or her whereabouts is unknown, the supervisor refuses to provide a reference, or no other individuals are able to provide information about the applicant's performance in a particular position.

What to Ask

Reference checkers usually don't set their sights high enough when making reference inquiries. They tend to assume that it is not worth the effort to ask former employers about the most important topics because of the popularity of restrictive reference policies. However, as the saying goes,

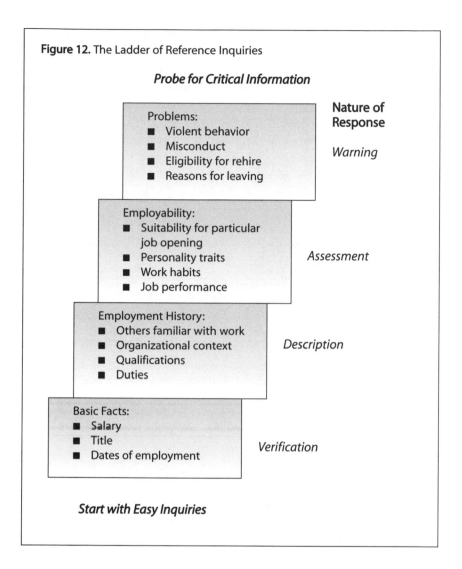

Figure 12. The Ladder of Reference Inquiries

Probe for Critical Information

Nature of Response

Problems:
- Violent behavior
- Misconduct
- Eligibility for rehire
- Reasons for leaving

Warning

Employability:
- Suitability for particular job opening
- Personality traits
- Work habits
- Job performance

Assessment

Employment History:
- Others familiar with work
- Organizational context
- Qualifications
- Duties

Description

Basic Facts:
- Salary
- Title
- Dates of employment

Verification

Start with Easy Inquiries

it never hurts to ask. Reference seekers may be surprised at the information they can discover about applicants if they ask the right questions in the right way. One thing is certain: If you don't ask, chances are that references won't tell you what you need to know about the applicant.

Conducting effective reference checks is like climbing a ladder (Figure 12). It involves ascending several rungs of increasingly higher-level inquiries, moving from questions that elicit verification of basic facts, to descriptions of various aspects of employment history, to assessments of issues relating to overall employability, to warnings about problem behaviors. At lower rungs of the reference inquiry ladder, it is easier to obtain information from a reference source. As reference checkers ascend the ladder, more skill is required to get information, but this information is more valuable to the potential employer in determining an applicant's fitness for a particular position and avoiding negligent hiring claims.

Reference checkers should use a standardized form and questions for conducting telephone reference checks for particular positions. A sample form that contains questions in each of the four categories on the ladder of reference inquiries appears earlier in this chapter.

Making the Call

Reference calls will be far more effective if the reference checker can structure calls and use techniques to communicate skillfully with reference sources. During the call the checker should focus on three things—establishing rapport, obtaining information, and leaving the door open for future inquiries.

1. **Establish rapport.** Your initial statements set the tone for the call. In the first minute of the conversation, strive to create a positive, professional, courteous impression. Your goal is to begin the call in a way that captures the recipient's attention and does not make him or her irritated or defensive.

   To start your call on the right note, introduce yourself and make a connection among you, the applicant, and the reference. Let the reference know that the applicant has given you permission to contact the reference. Make sure the reference is able to talk and does not feel inconvenienced by the interruption. So, you might begin the conversation as follows:

   YOU: *Hello, may I speak to Ann Jones?*
   MS. JONES: *This is Ann Jones.*

   YOU: *Ms. Jones, my name is _____. I am the human resource manager with ABC Company. I am calling in regard to Bill Smith, who has applied for a position in our _____ department. Bill mentioned that you supervised him when he worked at XYZ, Inc.,*

and gave his permission to contact you. Would this be a convenient time for us to talk for a few minutes about Bill?
MS. JONES: *Yes. (If the time is inconvenient, reschedule the call for a time convenient to the reference.)*

Avoid using the words "reference" or "employment verification" in your introductory statement, or you may put the source on the defensive or get referred to the human resources department.

Before you start asking questions, it's important to set the stage for cooperation from your reference source. After making your introduction, you should explain the purpose of your call in a way that will encourage cooperation instead of a fear of potential personal liability. Emphasize that an important reason for your inquiry is to obtain guidance on how to supervise the person most effectively in the event he or she is hired. A future focus and a little flattery will go a long way toward getting a reference to speak freely:

YOU: *Bill made several favorable comments about the guidance and direction he received from you when he worked for you. I want to be fair to Bill and make sure he would be a good fit for the job and our company. It would really help Bill and me if you could share some of your observations as to his ability to succeed in our organization.*

At this point, it is helpful to share pertinent information about your company and the job for which the applicant is being considered. These details will enable the reference to more accurately assess the applicant's suitability for the position.

YOU: *ABC Company is a company that _____ [describe what products or services your organization provides]. Our environment is _____ [describe a few key aspects of your company's culture and work environment]. We're considering Bill for a job in the _____ department, where he would be responsible for _____ [describe a few of the primary duties of the position].*

2. **Ask, listen, probe.** Once you have set the stage for cooperation, it's time to gather information from the source. To do this effectively, ask your questions, listen carefully, and probe for more details as needed.

Using your reference check form, start with the simple questions that merely require confirmation of basic facts. Then ask questions that seek more in-depth responses about employment history, job performance, and suitability for the position. Save the touchy questions relating to discipline, serious misconduct, and potential for violent behavior until after you have covered less sensitive topics. Record the source's responses on the reference check form. The reference checker's comments or observations relating to the call should be recorded on a separate area of the form.

As a general rule, ask open-ended questions to elicit full responses instead of "yes" or "no" replies. Open-ended questions often begin with the words "what" or "why" or phrases such as "tell me about" or "please describe."

Examples:

- *What were Bill's duties when he worked for you?*
- *Why did Bill leave XYZ Inc.?*
- *Tell me about Bill's ability to work with other people.*
- *Please describe any performance or discipline problems you had with Bill.*

There are certain circumstances where closed questions are helpful. Closed questions require "yes," "no," or brief responses. The closed-question format is useful to verify basic facts or to pinpoint specific details when a reference has given or is likely to give a vague response.

Examples:

- *Did Bill earn $_____ per _____ when he left your organization?*
- *What was Bill's title?*
- *Here is how Bill described his duties on his résumé. Is this an accurate description?*
- *Was Bill ever investigated or disciplined for serious misconduct?*
- *Did Bill ever exhibit violent or dangerous behaviors?*

Listen carefully and actively to the responses to these questions. Periodically, provide verbal feedback and probe for more information on particular topics. For instance, you might say, "That's interesting. Could you tell me more about that?" or "I see. Did Bill ever demonstrate those skills on other projects?"

"Scale" questions are another technique that can be used to probe for a concrete response. Let's say you asked a former supervisor, "How would you describe Bill's overall performance when he worked for you?" and the supervisor replied, "Bill was a good employee." This response is fairly vague, so you might follow up on this response by inquiring, "On a scale of 1 to 10, with 10 being the best, how would you rate Bill's overall performance?"

To confirm your understanding of what the source has told you, periodically restate or paraphrase the responses given. For example, after the source has described the applicant's reason for leaving, you might say, "So, Bill left your company for an opportunity to become a supervisor at EFG Ltd.?"

Well-timed pauses can also facilitate fuller disclosures. Don't assume a reference has a ready answer to every question. After you've asked a question, allow the source time to think and recall details. Wait for the response; otherwise, you may prompt a cursory reply. When you've asked a question and you've received a general or evasive reply, postpone your reply. Deliberate silences will invite further comments and explanations.

3. **Close the call.** After you've covered all the inquiries on the reference form, it's time to end the call gracefully and effectively. The last few sentences of your conversation should be used to thank the reference and invite future contact. For instance, you might conclude by saying:

YOU: *Ann, thanks so much for your comments about Bill. You've been very helpful. If you think of any other information that would assist us in evaluating or working with Bill, please feel free to contact me. My telephone number is _____.*

MS. JONES: *I think we've covered everything important, but I'll call you if I think of anything else.*

YOU: *That's great. Again, I really appreciate your assistance.*

Dealing with the Reluctant Source

Most reference sources will readily verify basic employment information but may be hesitant to answer other questions, particularly those relating to problems. Expect resistance to some questions and be ready to overcome it in a polite, yet persistent, way.

At the first sign of reluctance, offer to read or send the source a copy of the applicant's written reference authorization. Emphasize that this document includes a waiver of liability that protects the source and his or her organization. Reassure the source that information furnished will be held in confidence.

If you are talking to someone in an organization located in one of the thirty-five states that has a job reference immunity statute, mention this law and describe the protection it provides. Offer to provide a copy of this law if the reference is skeptical of its existence or applicability.

If the reference still refuses to disclose anything other than "name, rank, and serial number," explain that the applicant will not be hired unless you can obtain information about the individual's work experience and job performance from his or her current and recent employers. This technique may be particularly helpful in getting supervisors to open up about good former employees.

If the reference source still refuses to answer substantive questions, ask whether his or her failure to discuss your questions can be taken as an indication of problems with that employee. The way the source responds to this surprise question is likely to be telling. If the person ignores the question, or seems hesitant and nervous about answering, it may be because he or she does not want to share details about problems relating to the former employee. However, if the reference emphatically denies hiding any problems or plainly states that the sole reason for not answering questions is his or her organization's strict reference policy, this suggests that the employee in question was not a problem.

When the above strategies are not effective, try calling someone higher up and pleading your case again.

Perhaps in response to the challenges inherent in obtaining information about job performance, some employers have adopted a "non-check reference check." This approach involves calling all of the references at a time when they are likely to be out of their offices (for example, early in the morning, during the lunch hour, or in the evening). The caller leaves a message for the employers to call back *only* if they strongly recommend the applicant for the new position.

The theory behind the "non-check reference check" is that the fewer return calls, the greater the cause for concern about the applicant. This method may avoid confronting former employers with the need to give negative reference information. However, such "non-checks" may give inconsistent or misleading results. Calls may not be returned because of factors that are unrelated to the applicant's past performance and are beyond his or her control (such as supervisors who are out of the office or who do not return voice mail messages).

You've Got References—Now What?

Once reference checks have been completed, they should be used appropriately in employee selection and rejection. After hiring decisions have been made, reference records should be maintained and retained as required by law and company policy.

Evaluating References

If contradictory information surfaces during the reference-checking process, it is important to clear up the discrepancies. Either call additional references or call back the conflicting references and ask them for additional information about the issue in question. When evaluating disparate references, keep in mind how long and how well each reference source has known the candidate. The most credible reference sources will give a balanced view and won't focus exclusively on either all positive or all negative characteristics about the individual.

An unfavorable reference should not automatically eliminate an otherwise qualified candidate. Sometimes, negative comments may be the result of a grudge rather than the candidate's actual job performance. A former boss may give a bad reference because he or she is upset that a good employee has "deserted" the boss. If the candidate appears to be a good fit for the job and you suspect that the former supervisor is trying to get even, you may need to call others at the same organization to discover whether the supervisor's comments are motivated by valid performance issues or a grudge.

Inquiries by Rejected Applicants

A rejected applicant may assume (correctly or incorrectly) that his or her rejection resulted from a bad reference. Sometimes these applicants may contact the employer to find out who was contacted for a reference and what the references said. In these circumstances, respond to the applicant cordially, tactfully, and firmly. Acknowledge the applicant's feelings about being rejected and redirect the conversation in a more positive direction. For instance, you could say:

"I understand that it must be disappointing that you weren't selected for this position. You obviously have a lot to offer. However, we had many applicants for this job and we selected the individual we thought was best qualified. We will be happy to keep your application on file for ___ months, and we will consider you for future appropriate openings."

If the applicant continues to ask about his or her references after this statement, your fallback position should be to explain:

"I understand your interest in finding out about your references, but company policy prevents me from giving this information to any applicant."

Rephrase and repeat the company's policy, several times if necessary, if the applicant persists:

"Our policy strictly prohibits the release of any reference information."
"I am not allowed to discuss references under any circumstances, and may be disciplined for doing so."

Record Keeping

Employers must retain reference records for at least the minimum holding period established under federal, state, or local laws. If more than one law applies to the employer, and these laws have different record retention requirements, the employer must keep the records for the longer period.

Title VII of the Civil Rights Act of 1964, the Age Discrimination in Employment Act, and the Americans with Disabilities Act of 1990 require that records relating to employment decisions be kept for a minimum of one year after the record is made or action is taken, whichever is later. If a discrimination charge or lawsuit is filed, all relevant records must be maintained until final disposition.

The minimum retention period is two years for covered federal contractors under Executive Order 11246, the Rehabilitation Act of 1973, and the Vietnam Era Veterans' Readjustment Assistance Act.

Employers should inquire about record-keeping requirements in the states and municipalities in which they are located. State and local laws may establish longer minimum record-holding periods than required under federal law.

The content of reference discussions and records made during reference inquiries is private and may be sensitive. This information should not be shared with either applicants or employees. To do so is to breach implicit or explicit promises of confidentiality made to reference sources. Such practices may also open the door to legal problems for the employer, former employers, or individuals who gave references.

Reference documentation for rejected applicants should be kept with other applicant records. Reference records for employees should be kept in a confidential file that is separate from the employee's general history file because this file may be accessible to the employee under state law or company policy.

30 Tips for Getting References

The following "tip list" may help keep reference-getters on the right track.

1. Consider adopting a strict policy not to hire any individual unless a minimum number of satisfactory references are obtained.

2. Include in the documentation for applications a statement that a background check will be conducted prior to hire and that providing false information on the application form or during the application process is grounds for dismissal.

3. Require applicants to complete an authorization form permitting the company to conduct reference and background checks and containing a clear waiver of liability against your organization and agents and former and prospective employers and their agents for information given in a reference check.

4. Ask applicants to list specific periods of unemployment on the application.

5. Ask for all names ever used by an applicant.

6. Advise applicants in the interview that you will check their references.

7. During the interview, identify and gather names of several job-related references not listed on the candidate's own reference list.

8. Ask applicants to name individuals who should not be contacted for a reference and have them explain why.

9. Find out if the applicant is acquainted with any employees in your organization and ask these employees' opinions about the applicant.

10. Ask applicants to sign a statement as to the truthfulness of their answers to interview questions.

11. Have applicants assist in the reference-checking process by making necessary arrangements for you to talk with references you choose. This puts the burden on applicants to ensure that these references are obtained.

12. Ask applicants to provide copies of past performance reviews.

13. Conduct reference checks as the last step of the hiring process.

14. Don't rely solely on written references presented by the candidate.

15. Consider using a qualified outside firm to check references, especially for sensitive and upper-level positions.

16. Be sure to verify school attendance, degrees, and licenses as required for the position.

17. Check references by phone or in person. The response rate to written requests is lower.

18. Don't limit your reference contacts to those provided by the applicant.

19. Check more than one reference.

20. Document every reference contacted, even if the individual contacted refused to provide reference information.

21. Develop a broad network of contacts to open up informal sources of reference checking.

22. Avoid contacting the human resources department for references, unless there are no other contacts from the organization.

23. Remember that the higher up you go in a company's hierarchy, the more candid the responses are likely to be to reference inquiries.

24. When making telephone reference checks, start with the simple questions first.

25. Ask open-ended questions about employment history, job performance, and potential problems.

26. Never ask questions relating to age, race, sex, religion, national origin, or disability.

27. As appropriate for particular positions, check a prospective employee's criminal history, driving record, credit standing, and Social Security number.

28. Evaluate negative references fairly. A negative response from one individual doesn't necessarily mean the candidate is unqualified or difficult to work with.

29. Keep reference documentation confidential.

30. Retain reference records for at least the minimum period required by law.

CHAPTER 5

Practicalities: Getting References with Help from the Pros

Inside or Outside: Upsides and Downsides

While it is common for employers to take the "do-it-yourself" approach to investigating applicants, others outsource this task. According to the SHRM 1998 reference-checking survey, 15% of respondent employers used a third party to perform reference checks. Outside professionals are used more frequently for other types of pre-employment screening activities than they are for reference checks. The *Human Resource Executive*/ERC Dataplus 2000 background check poll found that 18% of employers polled used investigation firms to conduct in-depth background checks and 30% used other third-party vendors for simple, quick background checks.

Should your organization conduct employee screening internally or hire outside professionals? There are upsides and downsides to each approach (Table 6). Handling reference and background checks in-house means that your organization will have greater control over the administration of these activities, immediate access to information obtained, and precise knowledge of where and how information was obtained. In addition, the direct cost of conducting screening activities is typically lower when done internally. However, doing these checks internally may be inefficient and may slow down the hiring process unless your company has staff with expertise in background investigations. Moreover, if the staff responsible for the screening activities also meets the candidates during the hiring process, subjective biases may come into play in the evaluation of references or background check data.

Table 6. Internal vs. External Screening

Internal Screening
- **Advantages**
  Internal administrative control
  Immediate access to information
  Knowledge of exact procedures used to collect information
  Lower direct costs
  No FCRA compliance required

- **Disadvantages**
  Possible lack of staff expertise
  Possible lack of staff time to conduct checks
  Can slow down hiring process
  Handling of process may be inconsistent

External Screening
- **Advantages**
  Expertise and consistency in screening techniques
  Knowledge of applicable laws
  Familiarity with relevant records and databases
  Speed in obtaining information
  Convenience
  Objectivity of assessors
  Employers protected by FCRA's "qualified immunity" provisions

- **Disadvantages**
  Higher direct costs
  Less internal administrative control
  Employers are legally responsible for acts of third-party agents
  Must comply with the FCRA

Employers often find it more convenient or effective to outsource some or all pre-employment screening tasks. Key benefits of using capable, professional, third-party firms include their expertise in investigation techniques and knowledge of relevant federal and state laws. They will also be familiar with the methods of accessing various relevant databases across the country. Consequently, pre-employment screening firms usually are able to obtain information or provide the employer with online database access more speedily than the employer's staff. Another advantage of using outside firms is that they tend to be objective in evaluating information, since those doing reference checks, investigations, or reports have not met the subject and do not have a vested interest in whether a particular candidate is hired. Furthermore, use of third-party firms can ensure consistency in how the checks are handled and may be especially useful in this regard when the employer has multiple locations or a decentralized hiring process, or if hiring takes place on a cyclical basis and the employer does not need ongoing screening expertise.

Nevertheless, employers may not wish to use outside agencies to perform applicant screening duties because of budgetary constraints or because they wish to maintain total internal control of all aspects of the staffing process.

Moreover, employers may choose to handle applicant investigations internally so that they will not be subject to Fair Credit Reporting Act (FCRA) requirements for obtaining consumer reports from third parties. In spite of these additional administrative burdens imposed on employers, however, there is a distinct benefit to third-party pre-employment screening activities that are subject to the FCRA. A provision of the FCRA essentially creates qualified immunity for employers by prohibiting defamation, invasion of privacy, or negligence actions based on information disclosed in compliance with the FCRA, unless malice or willful intent to injure the consumer is shown.

Services, Services, and More Services

External reference and background checking services offer a smorgasbord of investigation and information services from which employers can choose according to their needs and budgets.

Pre-employment screening firms package their service options in a variety of ways (Figure 13). Firms differ significantly in the types of information they provide and how this information is obtained and delivered. Some companies offer a range of reference and background check services, and a few even offer psychological or cognitive assessments in their menu of services. Other companies specialize in providing particular types of information, such as credit reports or reference checks only. Some firms are full-service investigation agencies while others are strictly Web site operations that sell data at low cost. Depending on the service provider, screening information and reports may be made available to employers online, via written or telephone reports, or using a combination of these methods.

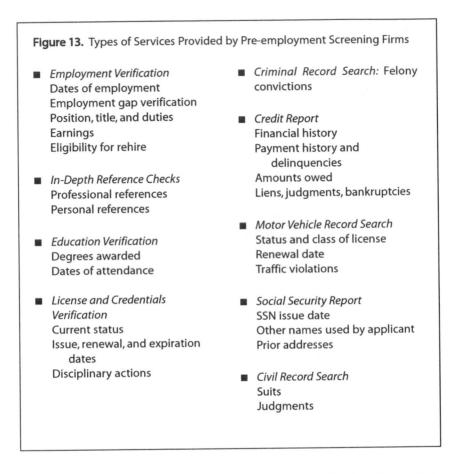

Figure 13. Types of Services Provided by Pre-employment Screening Firms

- *Employment Verification*
  Dates of employment
  Employment gap verification
  Position, title, and duties
  Earnings
  Eligibility for rehire

- *In-Depth Reference Checks*
  Professional references
  Personal references

- *Education Verification*
  Degrees awarded
  Dates of attendance

- *License and Credentials Verification*
  Current status
  Issue, renewal, and expiration dates
  Disciplinary actions

- *Criminal Record Search:* Felony convictions

- *Credit Report*
  Financial history
  Payment history and delinquencies
  Amounts owed
  Liens, judgments, bankruptcies

- *Motor Vehicle Record Search*
  Status and class of license
  Renewal date
  Traffic violations

- *Social Security Report*
  SSN issue date
  Other names used by applicant
  Prior addresses

- *Civil Record Search*
  Suits
  Judgments

Reference checking can be provided on two distinct levels. One widely available category of reference check service involves just verification of basic facts, such as dates of employment, employment gaps, positions held, and earnings. A second type of reference service that fewer firms offer is in-depth interviewing of professional or personal references that moves beyond mere facts verification and covers such topics as job performance, work habits, character and personality traits, and potential for violence.

Figure 14. Seven "C-crets" for Selecting a Screening Firm

1. *Compliance* with FCRA and other laws

2. *Confidentiality* is protected

3. *Correct and current* information provided

4. *Comprehensiveness* of services provided

5. *Completion time* for checks requested

6. *Cost* is competitive and affordable

7. *Client satisfaction* history and guarantees

The Choice Is Yours: Selecting the Right Screening Firm

The number of pre-employment screening firms has increased dramatically in recent years as employers have become increasingly concerned about negligent hiring lawsuits and as more public records have become available on the Internet.

According to industry experts, only a few companies offered pre-employment screening services in the early 1980s, but now there are hundreds of such firms. Much of this growth is attributable to "data warehouse" firms that only provide online database information to employers.

If you decide to outsource reference or background check responsibilities, consider the "C-crets" to selecting a firm shown in Figure 14.

1. Compliance

- Does the firm provide information to you and the subjects in compliance with the FCRA and other applicable federal and state laws?
- Does the firm have standard forms your organization can use to comply with the FCRA and other pertinent laws?

2. Confidentiality

- Does the firm have adequate procedures to ensure the confidentiality of the information?
- If reports are available online, how is access to the system secured and how are transmissions encrypted?

3. Current and Correct Information

- Is the supplied information the most current available?
- Does the information provided cover only the period permissible under the FCRA? (Generally, the FCRA does not allow third-party consumer reporting agencies to report information more than seven years old. An exception to this general rule allows screening firms to provide employers with information about criminal convictions that is more than seven years old. Another exception applies to information over seven years old that is to be used in connection with employment of an individual at an annual salary of $75,000 or more.)
- Does the firm review criminal records information and exclude arrest information before providing it to the employer?
- What safeguards does the firm take to ensure that information it supplies pertains to the correct individual rather than another individual with the same name?

4. Comprehensive Coverage

- Does the firm provide all of the screening services needed by your organization or will it be necessary to use more than one vendor?
- Does the firm have access to records from all states and available federal and county records? (Beware of firms that say they have access to a national criminal database. The only such database is the National Criminal Information Center database, which is available only to law enforcement agencies and employers in certain industries.)
- Is the firm able to tailor its services and forms to meet your company's special needs?

5. Completion Time

- How long will it take to receive information requested? Checks can be completed in a matter of days or even minutes, depending on the nature of the information needed and the firm's ability to provide the information quickly.
- If the firm provides "instantaneous" reports, does it have procedures in place to ensure that your company has complied with the FCRA requirements before you can access this information in real time? For example, some firms that promise the instantaneous online delivery of pre-employment screening information only do so after the employee has faxed them the required FCRA documentation.

- Employment verifications and reference checks can sometimes be obtained in one day, but they usually take three to five days to complete.
- Criminal records checks usually take several days to a week to obtain.
- The time it takes for screening firms to obtain motor vehicle records varies by state. A screening firm may be able to obtain a motor vehicle record within a day in many states, but in other states a driving history can take a week or more to obtain.

6. Cost

- What is the price for the services provided?
- How does the price compare to the price for similar services of competing firms? When evaluating costs, make sure to compare "apples to apples." Some firms may quote lower costs for a particular check, but provide less extensive or current information or a lower level of service. For example, the cost of reference checks can range from $10 to more than $300 depending on the types of information sought, the length and content of the report provided, and the number of individuals contacted. The lower-priced checks are likely to be limited to basic fact checking, while the more expensive reference checks may include verbal and written reports of in-depth discussions with multiple reference sources. Similarly, costs of criminal history checks will vary based on the number of county and state records included in the search.

7. Client Satisfaction

- Has the firm provided similar reference or background check services to organizations in your industry?
- Is the firm willing to provide customer references for you to contact?
- What client satisfaction guarantees does the firm provide?
- Does the firm provide its clients with customer service, resource materials, or updates relating to legal and practical issues in pre-employment screening?

Appendix C provides a partial list of companies that offer pre-employment screening services.

The Fair Credit Reporting Act

Employers who outsource pre-employment screening activities must comply with the Fair Credit Reporting Act (FCRA). Failure to follow the requirements of this federal law exposes covered employers to potential civil liability that can include actual damages, litigation costs, and attorney's fees, as well as punitive damages for willful violations. The FCRA also contains criminal penalties including fines and imprisonment for any person who knowingly and willfully obtains information on a consumer from a consumer reporting agency under false pretenses.

FCRA Applicability to Employment Screening

Some employers mistakenly assume that the FCRA requirements apply only to credit reports obtained from credit bureaus. The scope of the FCRA is actually much broader; it requires that any employer requesting a "consumer report" or an "investigative consumer report" for employment purposes from a third-party "consumer reporting agency" must comply with certain disclosure and adverse action requirements. If an employer uses its own staff to perform pre-employment screening activities, it does not have to comply with the FCRA.

A "consumer reporting agency" includes any person or company that regularly assembles or evaluates information about individuals for the purpose of furnishing a consumer report and charges a fee to the user of the report. Thus, the FCRA's definition of consumer reporting agency applies to private investigators, third-party public records providers, and online database companies who provide consumer reports to employers. The FCRA does not apply to situations where an employer obtains public records directly from a government agency.

The term "consumer report" covers any written, oral, or other communication bearing on a consumer's creditworthiness, credit standing, credit capacity, character, general reputation, personal characteristics, or mode of living that is used or expected to be used for employment purposes. Therefore, consumer reports include not only credit reports, but also criminal records checks, reference checks, motor vehicle reports, and verification of education and licenses.

An "investigative consumer report" is a type of consumer report or portion of a consumer report in which personal interviews with neighbors, friends, associates, or other acquaintances are used to obtain information on an individual's character, general reputation, personal characteristics, or mode of living. The difference between an investigative consumer report and a consumer report is that information for investigative consumer reports has been gathered by talking to people. Users of investigative consumer reports must comply with additional FCRA requirements.

Disclosure Requirements

Before an employer can obtain a consumer report about a job applicant or an employee from third parties in conjunction with pre-employment screening activities, the FCRA requires that the employer

- provide written disclosure to the applicant or employee that a consumer report may be obtained;
- obtain written authorization from the applicant or the employee; and
- certify to the consumer reporting agency that it is in compliance with the FCRA.

There are additional requirements for investigative consumer reports. Within three days of requesting an investigative consumer report, the employer must 1) provide written disclosure to the individual that an investigative consumer report may be made; 2) inform the individual of the right to request disclosures about the nature and scope of the investigation; and 3) provide a written summary of the individual's rights under the FCRA.

Adverse Action Requirements

The FCRA does not prohibit employers from taking an adverse action, such as rejecting an applicant, based on information contained in a consumer report, but it does mandate that the employer comply with the following requirements.

- Before the adverse action is taken, the employer must provide the applicant or employee with a copy of the consumer report and a summary of rights under the FCRA.
- After the adverse action is taken, the employer must provide the applicant or employee with notice of the adverse action, contact information for the consumer reporting agency that furnished the report, a statement that the consumer reporting agency did not make the adverse action decision and is unable to provide reasons for the adverse

action, and notice of the rights to obtain a free copy of the consumer report and to dispute the accuracy or completeness of information contained in the consumer report.

Special FCRA procedures apply to the trucking industry. Employers do not have to make written disclosures or obtain written permission before obtaining a consumer report on applicants who will be subject to state or federal regulations for commercial truck drivers and who have applied for such positions by mail, telephone, or computer. Instead, the required FCRA notice and consent may be handled orally or electronically. Nor is the employer required to provide pre-adverse-action disclosures to these individuals. Instead the employer must provide oral, written, or electronic adverse action disclosures within three days of the decision.

When Reference Checks Are Not Subject to FCRA Requirements

A reference check conducted by a consumer reporting agency may constitute an investigative consumer report unless it satisfies conditions that specifically exclude it from the FCRA "consumer report" definition. As long as a reference report furnished to an employer by a third party is used only for employment purposes, and the employer has obtained the candidate's consent to check references, the report is an excluded communication that is not subject to the FCRA's notice and adverse action requirements for investigative consumer reports.

Under this exclusion, if a candidate asks to see a reference report, the reference-checking firm is required to provide him or her with a written disclosure of the nature and substance of the information in the candidate's file within five business days of the request; in such circumstances, however, the reference-checking firm would not be required to disclose the reference sources. In addition, the reference-checking firm must provide the candidate with written notice of the candidate's right to request this information.

Notwithstanding this excluded-communication exemption from the FCRA, some reference-checking firms still choose to comply with FCRA requirements for investigative consumer reports when conducting reference checks.

State Credit Check Laws

Some states have enacted their own fair credit laws. Most of these laws are modeled after the FCRA. State credit check laws vary in certain areas including the use of consumer reports for employment purposes, adverse action notice requirements, and the information available to applicants.

The FCRA does not exempt employers from complying with applicable state credit check laws, but the FCRA takes precedence in many instances where provisions of state laws are inconsistent with the FCRA. Even in these instances, however, the FCRA provides that it does not apply to any provision of state law enacted after January 1, 2004, that is explicitly intended to supplement federal requirements and that gives greater protection to consumers than the FCRA.

CHAPTER 6

Practicalities: Reference Checking in Your Organization

A New Beginning for Your Reference-Checking Program?

Chapters 1 through 5 of this book described the truths and consequences of giving and getting references in today's workplaces. As has been shown, legal issues abound, and there are a myriad of potential legal and practical pitfalls for unwary employers. To complicate matters further, various federal, state, and local laws affect or restrict the ways employers can conduct reference checks and other pre-employment screening activities.

Naturally, employers have been concerned about the possible liabilities associated with reference checking, especially with giving references. Consequently, many employers have developed strict "no comment" or "name, rank, and serial number" reference policies that protect them from lawsuits, but with significant costs or difficulties for themselves, their good employees, and other employers. Because of the prevalence of restrictive reference disclosure policies, employers often experience frustration when the tables are turned and they attempt to obtain information about an applicant's work history and job performance from former employers.

While it is not easy for employers on either side of the reference-checking table, there are many steps that employers can take both to minimize the risks and to maximize the usefulness of reference checks. These two objectives are not mutually exclusive. All it takes is knowledge of safe and effective reference-checking strategies and a willingness to implement them.

Taking a Second Look at Your Reference-Checking Practices

The following worksheet (Figure 15) can be used to evaluate your current reference-checking program and to pinpoint areas in which it can be improved.

Figure 15. Evaluating and Designing a Reference-Checking Program

Part 1: Giving References

Suggested Practice	In Place	Implement	Consider	Not Applicable
Develop a written policy that specifies procedures for giving references about current or former employees				
Review written policy with supervisors				
Include the reference policy in the employee handbook				
Review the reference policy with employees at termination				
Tell discharged employees the real reasons for termination (to minimize risk of compelled self-publication and wrongful discharge claims)				
Develop reference authorization form				
Establish a policy not to provide any references unless the (former) employee has first signed a reference authorization form				

Suggested Practice	In Place	Implement	Consider	Not Applicable
Establish a policy prohibiting supervisors from preparing "to whom it may concern" recommendation letters				
Establish guidelines as to who may provide references (human resources staff? supervisors? others?)				
Train human resources staff, supervisors, and other appropriate parties on proper methods for handling reference contacts				
Provide references only in response to valid inquiries				
Establish guidelines on the specific types of information that may be given in response to a reference request				
Establish guidelines for responding to inquiries about (former) employees who are potentially violent				
Develop a form for documenting reference requests				
Require documentation of responses to every reference request (whether or not any information is provided to the requester) *continued next page*				

Figure 15 *continued*. Evaluating and Designing a Reference-Checking Program

Suggested Practice	In Place	Implement	Consider	Not Applicable
Maintain reference documentation in a confidential employee file				
Restrict access to reference documentation to individuals who have a valid need to know the information				
Retain reference documentation for at least the minimum periods required by law				

Part 2: Getting References				
Suggested Practice	In Place	Implement	Consider	Not Applicable
Establish minimum pre-employment screening requirements for all positions				
Identify high-risk jobs and establish appropriate screening requirements for these jobs				
Adopt a requirement that no individual will be hired without satisfactory references				

Suggested Practice	In Place	Implement	Consider	Not Applicable
Develop a written policy that specifies the procedures for obtaining references about candidates for open positions				
Include a statement on the application form that notifies applicants of possible reference and background checks				
Include a statement on the application form that giving false information is grounds for rejection or discharge				
Design application form to include space for applicants to provide information about all names used, Social Security number, and periods of unemployment				
Include signature and date line on application				
Train those who screen applications to watch for "red flags"				
Develop an applicant reference authorization form				
Establish a policy not to obtain any references unless candidate has signed a reference authorization form *continued next page*				

Figure 15 *continued*. Evaluating and Designing a Reference-Checking Program

Suggested Practice	In Place	Implement	Consider	Not Applicable
Develop a standard form to document all reference contacts and their out-comes				
Require applicants to complete the application and reference authoriza-tion form on-site				
Provide applicants with a written notice of the organization's policy on the accuracy of applica-tion information				
Require applicants to review their application for completeness and accuracy before submis-sion				
Require interviewees to bring a check stub, cur-rent business card, and copies of any required licenses or degrees to the interview				
Identify the names of additional reference sources during the interview				
During the interview, determine parties that the candidate does not want to be contacted and find out why				

Suggested Practice	In Place	Implement	Consider	Not Applicable
Ask applicants to provide copies of past performance appraisals				
Ask applicants to set up reference calls				
Determine whether references will be checked by telephone, mail, fax, e-mail, or in person				
Conduct reference checks as the last step in the hiring process				
Designate responsibility for conducting reference checks (human resources? supervisors? third-party service provider?)				
If reference checks are to be outsourced, select appropriate provider(s)				
Determine topics to be addressed in reference checks (go beyond basic facts verification)				
Develop a reference check form that includes questions to be asked by reference checkers				
Train reference checkers in effective reference-checking techniques				

continued next page

Figure 15 *continued*. Evaluating and Designing a Reference-Checking Program

Suggested Practice	In Place	Implement	Consider	Not Applicable
Document all reference contacts, regardless of whether a reference was provided				
Develop guidelines for evaluating references				
Train human resources staff and managers in methods of handling inquiries by rejected applicants				
Develop record-keeping procedures to maintain confidentiality of reference documentation				
Maintain reference documentation in a confidential file separate from normal personnel files				
Restrict access to reference documentation to individuals who have a valid need to know the information				
Retain reference documentation for at least minimum periods required by law				

Answers to "Test Your Knowledge of Legal Issues," Chapter 2

1. **Employers have a duty to provide information about former employees' dates of employment, positions held, earnings, and job performances, upon request from any third party.**

   FALSE. While it is permissible and helpful to provide this information to prospective employers, it is risky to provide job references to anyone and everyone who requests them. References should be given only to parties who have a legitimate need for the information. To do otherwise is to create potential liability for invasion of privacy. In addition, employers may potentially be liable for defamatory statements made to parties who do not have a valid need for the information.

2. **It is inadvisable to comment on the applicant's sexual preference unless specifically asked about that by the prospective employer.**

   FALSE. It would be inadvisable regardless of whether the prospective employer specifically asks about sexual preference. Disclosure of such information could give rise to a suit for invasion of privacy against both the reference giver and the potential employer. Sex discrimination claims are also possible if the reference is given in a state or municipality that prohibits discrimination based on sexual preference.

3. **As long as an employer provides only positive information about former employees, it can avoid potential legal liability.**

   FALSE. Providing positive but misleading references about former employees who have harmful tendencies may provide the basis for a misrepresentation lawsuit.

4. In certain situations, an employer will not be liable for defamation when a supervisor makes false statements about a former employee.

   TRUE. An employer will not be liable for defamation in situations where the employee has given consent and has released the employer from liability for providing a reference, the defamatory statements are protected by qualified privilege, or the state has a job reference immunity law that the employer has followed.

5. Employers should not provide references for former employees who have filed discrimination claims.

   FALSE. If the organization typically provides references for former employees, to not do so because the employee exercised rights granted by federal or state discrimination laws could be viewed as illegal retaliation. Similarly, it would also be considered retaliatory to give a bad reference about a former employee for the purpose of getting even with the employee for filing a discrimination claim.

6. Employers do not have to conduct the same number of reference checks for all candidates for the same position.

   TRUE. There is no law that requires employers to check the same number of references for candidates for the same job. However, to avoid potential disparate treatment discrimination claims, employers should check the same number of references at the same stage of the hiring process for all candidates for a particular position. If there is a sound business reason to check a different number of references for a particular candidate (such as in instances where the candidate's references are contradictory), then variations in the number of references checked for different candidates are legally justifiable.

7. Employers have a duty to make a reasonable investigation of an individual's background before hiring that person.

   TRUE. An employer may be potentially liable for negligent hiring if it hires an unsuitable individual without adequately investigating that person's background and that individual harms others while on the job.

8. If a former supervisor reveals information relating to an applicant's current pregnancy during a reference check, the potential employer should document this information so that it can be used in discussing scheduling issues.

   FALSE. If a reference checker hears information relating to characteristics such as pregnancy that are protected under federal or state laws, the reference checker should not record, repeat, or rely on the information for the purpose of making an employment decision.

9. It is permissible to inquire whether a candidate has filed a charge of discrimination because such information is job-related.

   FALSE. It is impermissible to discriminate in hiring against persons who have exercised their rights under federal civil rights laws.

10. The Fair Credit Reporting Act (FCRA) requires that employers who handle reference and background checks internally must obtain an applicant's prior written consent.

    FALSE. The FCRA applies to reference and background-checking activities performed by third-party consumer reporting agencies and is not applicable when such employee-screening activities are handled internally. However, to avoid potential legal liability for invasion of privacy and other torts, it is always advisable to obtain an applicant's authorization before conducting reference and background checks.

References: A European Perspective

by Elizabeth Gillow and Martin Hopkins, Eversheds*

AUTHOR'S NOTE

When giving or getting references outside of U.S. borders, employers should keep in mind that reference-checking laws and customs in other countries often can be quite different from those of the United States. Legislation and case law abroad may focus on similar legal issues (for example, defamation, discrimination, retaliation, or misrepresentation). However, the rights of employees and the employers' obligations and rights may vary considerably from those in the United States, and from country to country.

Some of these variations are highlighted in the following overview of reference-checking laws in countries of the European Union (EU) and the analysis of cases from the United Kingdom. Each EU country has its own laws and customs. Nevertheless, U.S. employers who seek references from EU employers—or who have European operations and employees— should be aware that EU countries generally are quite protective of employees' privacy and other rights in the workplace.

Before obtaining or providing job references in other countries, American employers should seek legal and practical guidance from a qualified professional who understands international law as well as the employment laws of the specific countries where the reference-checking activities will occur. Conversely, during the hiring process, U.S. employers who are interviewing applicants from other countries should understand that these candidates might have different expectations about references. The potential employer should clearly explain the company's expectations, policies, and practices regarding references, as well as the applicable state and federal legal requirements. —Wendy Bliss

References in Europe

A common misconception outside of Europe is that there is a federal legal system for all the Member States of the European Union (EU), with some minor variations in each individual country. This is not the case. Each EU country has a separate legal framework, with different origins, and only comparatively recently has the EU ordered each Member State to approximate the law in particular areas.

The laws relating to references have developed piecemeal in each Member State, although there are some similarities. Many of the EU countries require the employer or ex-employer to provide a certificate of employment, which gives the basic details such as dates of employment, the position(s) held, and (in some cases) current or latest salary. In Ireland, Spain, Sweden, and the United Kingdom (UK), there is no general statutory obligation to provide any sort of reference, but there may be an obligation under a collective agreement. In Spain there is an obligation to provide a reference for employees on a training contract or work experience. In Italy employees keep a booklet containing key employment information from all previous employers.

Only two of the EU Member States require employers to give full references—Germany and the Netherlands—but it is common in most other EU countries to provide a full reference on request. Some countries have restrictions as to what can be included. In France, for example, information that could prejudice an employer against an applicant should not be included even if factually correct. In Sweden, a reference must not refer to sickness, absence, or other legal leave. In all EU countries, the employer has a legal duty of care to the employee or the prospective employer—or both—and the employer will be liable for loss or damage caused by an inaccurate reference.

Examples from the UK

In practice, most UK employers do provide references for employees or ex-employees when requested to do so. However, there is no statutory obligation to provide a reference except in particular industries, such as the financial services sector. If a reference is provided it must not only be accurate but must also give a fair and balanced impression of the employee. This does not mean that a reference has to be bland and meaningless—but it must be reasonable and justifiable.

There are other occasions when an employee might have a right to a reference. One such instance is where an employee can claim that there is an implied contractual right because giving references is customary practice within an industry or profession. If this is the case, a refusal may amount to a breach of contract for which the individual can claim damages.

Another situation where a reference must be given is when it is part of an agreement on termination of employment. An example would be when the employer agrees to pay a certain severance sum and to provide an agreed-upon reference in exchange for the employee's leaving and agreeing not to press any employment-related claims.

There is no legislation in the UK relating specifically to references. However, there is case law that creates binding precedents and that all employers must take into account if they do give references.

The first case where an employer was held liable for a negligent reference is *Spring -v- Guardian Assurance plc.*[18] Mr. Spring worked in the financial services industry, where employers are required to provide a reference. The reference sent to Mr. Spring's prospective employer suggested that he consistently kept the best deals for himself, had little regard for the sales team he managed, was a man of little or no integrity, and could not be regarded as honest. Not surprisingly, his prospective employer withdrew the job offer. He subsequently failed to obtain employment with two other insurance companies.

Mr. Spring sought damages against Guardian on the basis that the reference was a negligent misstatement. The House of Lords held that an employer who provides a reference concerning an employee or a former employee owes a duty of care to the employee regarding the preparation and contents of the reference.

The duty of care that an employer owes to its employee was looked at again in *Bartholomew -v- London Borough of Hackney.*[19] Mr. Bartholomew was employed by Hackney Council. He was suspended pending an investigation into financial irregularities. During the course of his suspension, he brought a claim of race discrimination against the Council. The parties reached a settlement under which Mr. Bartholomew would take voluntary severance, with pay in lieu of notice, and that he would withdraw his complaint. The disciplinary action would be dropped on termination of employment.

Subsequently, the Council was asked for a reference by a prospective employer. The reference stated that Mr. Bartholomew had taken voluntary severance following the deletion of his post and that, at the time of leaving, he was "suspended from work due to a charge of gross misconduct and disciplinary action had commenced. This disciplinary action lapsed automatically on his departure from the authority." The prospective employer withdrew its offer. Mr. Bartholomew brought a claim for damages, alleging that his former employer had breached its duty of care by providing a reference that, though factually correct, was unfair.

The Court of Appeal concluded that Hackney Council did not breach its duty and that if the Council had not referred to the suspension at all, it might have been in breach of the duty of care to the prospective employer. The Court of Appeal went on to clarify what the duty consisted of: It is not enough for a reference to be factually correct; it must also give a fair and balanced impression of the employee.

Another case demonstrates that failure to give a reference may result in a claim: *Coote -v- Granada Hospitality*.[20] Ms. Coote managed a bowling center in East London. When she left, she brought a sex discrimination claim against Granada Hospitality on the grounds that she had been dismissed because of her pregnancy. The case was settled. Ms. Coote subsequently applied for other jobs, but Granada refused to provide a reference. She then brought a victimization claim on the basis that the refusal was directly because of her previous claim of sex discrimination. The Employment Appeal Tribunal concluded that Ms. Coote was entitled to damages for sex discrimination from her former employer, even though she was no longer in their employment.

In a parallel case under the Race Relations Act, the opposite conclusion was reached and the former employee was not entitled to damages for racial victimization. This is because the law on sex discrimination emanates from the EU Equal Treatment Directive, which was interpreted as requiring protection for former employees as well as current employees. There is no such directive relating to race discrimination, although this aspect of the Race Relations Act is likely to be brought into line with the Directive.

The effect of the ruling in *Coote* is not to require employers to provide references: It is to preclude employers from refusing to provide references with a view to penalizing an employee who has brought a sex discrimination (or equal pay) claim.

Elizabeth Gillow and Martin Hopkins can be reached at Eversheds, 115 Colmore Row, Birmingham B3 3AL, United Kingdom, Telephone: (011) 44-121-232-1000, Fax: (011) 44-121-232-1900, E-mail: elizabethgillow@eversheds.com or martinhopkins@eversheds.com

A Sample Listing of Firms Providing Pre-employment Screening Services

NOTE
This brief list is not inclusive and does not constitute an endorsement by the Society for Human Resource Management or the author. Before selecting a provider of reference or background check services, employers should contact and evaluate several such services.

AccuFacts Pre-Employment Screening, Inc.
6 Greene Street
2nd Floor
New York, NY 10013
(800) 955-5411
http://www.accufacts.com

Advantage Assessment, Inc.
Suite 30-A
15 West Strong Street
Pensacola, FL 32501
(800) 600-2510
http://www.advantageis.com

American Background Information Services, Inc.
629 Cedar Creek Grade
Suite C
Winchester, VA 22601
(800) 669-2247
http://www.americanbackground.com

Avert, Inc.
301 Remington Street
Fort Collins, CO 80524
(800) 367-5933
http://www.avert.com

Barada Associates, Inc.
130 East Second Street
Rushville, IN 46173
(765) 932-5917
http://www.baradainc.com

BTi Employee Screening Services, Inc.
8150 North Central Expressway
Suite 500
Dallas, TX 75206
(800) 658-5638
http://www.btiscreening.com

Certified Reference Checking Co.
1325 Lake St. Louis Blvd. #100
Lake St. Louis, MO 63367
(636) 561-4477

ChoicePoint, Inc.
1000 Alderman Drive
Alpharetta, GA 30005
(770) 752-5681
http://www.choicepointinc.com

CIC Applicant Background Checks
12505 Starkey Road
Suite K
Largo, FL 33773
(727) 535-4473
http://www.hirecheck.com

Equifax
1979 Lakeside Parkway
Suite 500
Tucker, GA 30004
(800) 456-6003
http://www.equifax.com

General Information Services, Inc.
120C Columbia Avenue
P.O. Box 353
Chapin, SC 29036
(888) GEN-INFO
http://www.geninfo.com

HRPlus
2902 Evergreen Parkway
Suite 100
Evergreen, CO 80439
(800) 332-PLUS
http://www.hrplus.com

InfoLink Screening Services
17609 Ventura Boulevard
Suite 210
Encino, CA 91316
(818) 990-4473
http://www.infolink-hire.com

InfoMart
1640 Powers Ferry Road
Building 19
Marietta, GA 30067
(800) 800-3774
http://www.ers.infomart-usa.com

Justifacts Credential Verification, Inc.
98 Devonshire Drive
P.O. Box 357
Delmont, PA 15626
(724) 468-5936
http://justifacts.com

LaborChex Companies
3900 Lakeland Drive
Suite 300
Jackson, MS 39208
(800) 880-0366
http://www.laborchex.com

On-Line Screening Services, Inc.
3135 SR 580
Suite 5
Safety Harbor, FL 34695
(800) 358-5383
http://www.onlinescreening.com

PeopleWise
2339 Technology Parkway
Suite F
Hollister, CA 95023
(800) 631-8777
http://www.people-wise.com

Pinkerton
15910 Ventura Boulevard
Suite 900
Encino, CA 91436
(800) 232-7465
http://www.pinkertons.com

Reid Psychological Systems
153 West Ohio Street
Chicago, IL 60610
(312) 938-9200
http://www.reidsystems.com

Robert Arden & Associates, Inc.
450 Skokie Boulevard
Suite 604
Northbrook, IL 60062
(847) 480-9050
http://www.robertarden.com

Sterling Testing Systems, Inc.
254 West 31st Street
6th Floor
New York, NY 10001
http://www.sterlingtesting.com

Trans Union Employment Screening Services, Inc.
611 Oak Tree Boulevard
Cleveland, OH 44131
(800) 853-3228
http://www.tuess.com

USA-FACT, Inc.
6200 Sycamore Canyon Boulevard
Suite A
Riverside, CA 92507
(909) 656-7800
http://www.usafact.com

Verifications, Inc.
920 Second Avenue South
Minneapolis, MN 55402
(800) 735-3002
http://www.verificationsinc.com

Notes

1. "Heart of Darkness," *People*, 10 April 2000, 205–210.

2. Alex Tresniowski, "Rx: Life Behind Bars," *People*, 9 October 2000, 74.

3. Todd Wallack, "Tall Tales from Oakland Startup Star," *San Francisco Chronicle*, 14 July 2000, A1.

4. *Randi W. v. Muroc Joint Unified School District*, 929 P.,2d 582 (Cal. 1997).

5. Society for Human Resource Management, *Reference Checking Handbook, revised edition* (Alexandria, VA: Society for Human Resource Management), 1994, 14.

6. Title VII of the Civil Rights Act of 1964 and the Americans with Disabilities Act apply to employers with fifteen or more employees; the Age Discrimination in Employment Act applies to employers with twenty or more employees. Smaller employers who are not subject to these federal laws still may be subject to the nondiscrimination provisions of state fair employment practices statutes, which may apply to employers with as few as one or two employees.

7. *Robinson v. Shell Oil Company*, 117 S.Ct. 483 (1997).

8. *Frank B. Hall & Co. Inc., v. Buck*, 678 S.W.2d 612 (Tex.App. 14 Dist. 1984).

9. *Irwin v. Wal-Mart Stores*, 6 IER Cases 975 (Mo. Ct. App. 1991).

10. Robert J. Nobile, *Guide to HR Policies and Procedures* (Boston: Warren, Gorham & Lamont) 1996, 8-32, citing *Jerner v. Allstate Insurance Company*, 650 So.2d 997 (2d Dist. 1995).

11. "Running Reference Check Roadblocks," *HR Focus*, November 1998, 5.

12. "Firms Giving References for Former Workers Choose to Remain Quiet-Perhaps Too Quiet," *Bulletin to Management*, 19 November 1998, 362.

13. "Poorly Treated Staff Are More Likely to Sue," *HR Briefing*, 10 October 1998, 2.

14. *Davis v. Ross*, 754 F.2d 80 (1985).

15. "Being Honest About Dishonesty," *HR Magazine*, September 2000, 29.

16. Michelle Dalton Liberatore, "Most Organizations Use Background Checks as Prescreening Tools," *Human Resource Executive*, 2 May 2000, 37.

17. Society for Human Resource Management, *Reference Checking*, 14.

18. [1999 IRLR 246]

19. [1998 IRLR 656]

20. [1994 IRLR 460]

Index

A

Absolute privilege, 19–20
"Ad hoc" approach to references, 35
Age Discrimination in Employment Act
  of 1967, 14, 16, 86
Allstate Insurance Company,
  misrepresentation case, 23
American Background Information
  Services, Inc., 6, 7
Americans with Disabilities Act of 1990,
  14, 16, 86
Applicant consent form, 64–66
Applicants
  enlisting their help in getting references,
    72–75
  rejected, 86, 87
  verifying truth of statements, 5–6
Application for employment, 63–64
Application process, 72–73
Arrest records. *See* Criminal records check
Avert, Inc., statistics from, 57, 59

B

Background checks
  legally mandated in some industries, 22,
    26
  outsourcing, 29
  when filling high-risk positions, 56–60
Bankruptcy, 58
*Bartholomew -v- London Borough of
  Hackney,* 117–18
Blacklisting laws, 31, 32
Buck, Larry, 18

C

Cases in point
  defamation cases, 17, 18, 19
  misrepresentation case, 23
  retaliation case, 15
Centralizing reference checking, 77
Checkpoint Systems Inc., dishonesty and
  theft on the job, study of, 55
Civil Rights Act of 1964. *See* Title VII of
  the Civil Rights Act of 1964
Clients and customers, suitability as
  references, 78
Confidential information/confidentiality
  issues
  contacting references, 76
  disclosing confidential information,
    21–22
  pre-employment screening firms, 95
  written, faxed, or e-mailed reference
    checks, 76
Consent of applicant or employee
  to disclose personnel information and
    release of liability, sample form, 40
  in getting references, 64–66
  legal protection through, 20–21
Consumer report, 93, 98
  investigative, 98–99, 100
Consumer reporting agencies, 98, 100
Contacting references
  confidentiality issues, 76
  dealing with reluctant sources, 84–85
  making the call, 80–83
  methods compared, 76–77
  "non-check reference check," 84–85

statistics, 76–77
timing, 77
what to ask, 78–80
whom to contact, 77–78
who should contact references, 77
Coote -v- Granada Hospitality, 118–19
Coworkers, suitability as references, 78
Credit checks, 58, 60
Criminal records checks, 57–58, 60

D

Dangerous tendencies, liability for not
    disclosing known information about,
    22–24
Defamation, 16–19
    qualified and absolute privileges and,
    19–20
Disability discrimination, 21
Discrimination, 14, 22, 26–29. *See also*
    Retaliation
inappropriate questions, 28
Disparate treatment discrimination
    claims, 14
Documentation and record keeping
    in getting references, 63–71, 86–87
    reference inquiries, 46–48
    retention of reference documentation,
    48–49, 86–87
Driving record checks, 59

E

Educational credentials, verifying, 55–56
EEO. *See* Federal equal employment
    opportunity laws
E-mailing references, 76
Employee Polygraph Protection Act, 16
Employee Retirement Income Security Act,
    16
Employee selection and rejection, use of
    reference checks in, 85–87
Employment application, 63–64
Employment history, verifying, 55
Equal Pay Act, 16
ERC Dataplus survey. *See Human
    Resource Executive* magazine/ERC
    Dataplus survey
EU Equal Treatment Directive, 118

Europe, perspective on legal issues in
    reference checking, 32, 115–19
Evaluating references, 85
Executive Order 11246, records retention,
    87
Expediting the process of extending job
    offers, 63

F

Fair Credit Reporting Act (FCRA), 29
    about, 29
    adverse action requirements, 99–100
    applicability to pre-employment
    screening, 98–99
    disclosure requirements, 99
    possible violations, 26
    state credit check laws, 100–101
    when checks are not subject to
    requirements, 100
Fair Labor Standards Act, 16
Falsified information/fabrications
    in getting references, 54–55
    statistics, 6
Family and Medical Leave Act, 16
Fast-track process of extending job offers,
    63
Fax transmission of references, 76
FCRA. *See* Fair Credit Reporting Act
Federal equal employment opportunity
    (EEO) laws, 14
Financial status of applicants, 58
Florida, negligent hiring safe harbor
    law, 26
Forms, notices, and policies, samples
    Sample Employee Consent to Disclose
    Personnel Information and Release
    of Liability, 40
    Sample General Policy on Checking
    References for All New Hires, 61
    Sample Notice to Job Applicants, 73
    Sample Policy on Providing Employment
    References, 37
    Sample Record of Employee Reference
    Form, 47
    Sample Reference-Checking Form, 67
Fortune 500 survey, time spent checking
    references, 77
France, reference laws in, 116

G

Georgia, negligent hiring law, 26
Germany, reference laws in, 116
Getting references. *See also* Pre-
  employment screening practices
  about, 53–54
  additional investigation in high-risk
    positions, 56–60
  application process, 72–73
  asking open-ended questions, 82–83
  contacting references, 76–85
  documentation and record keeping,
    63–71, 86–87
  enlisting applicant's help in, 72–75
  evaluating references, 85
  falsified information/fabrications, 54–55
  interview practices, 73–75
  ladder of reference inquiries, 79–80
  "non-check reference check," 84–85
  reality check, 9–10
  tips for, 87–89
  use in selection and rejection, 85–87
  written policy on, 60–63
Gillow, Elizabeth, 115
Giving references. *See also* Handling
    inquiries
  achieving balance in, 36–42
  "ad hoc" approach, 35
  balancing risk against offering helpful
    information, 33
  "name, rank, and serial number"
    approach, 34–35, 103
  "no comment" approach, 33–34, 103
  reality check, 8–9
  reckless reference case, 18
  reference authorization form, 21, 39–40
  reference policy, 36–38
  termination practices and, 41–42
  test your knowledge, 12–13, 111–13
  tips for, 49–51
  typical approaches, 33–36

H

Handling inquiries
  consistency in responding to inquiries,
    45–46
  documentation and record keeping,
    46–48

information that can be provided, 44–45
retention of reference documentation,
  48–49
to whom references should be given,
  43–44
who should give references, 42–43
High-risk positions, 56–60
Hopkins, Martin, 115
Horror stories, 3–4, 25
Human Resource Executive
    magazine/ERC Dataplus survey
  criminal and credit checks, 57, 58
  motor vehicle record checks, 59
  Social Security Number verification, 59
  use of outside agencies, 91
Human resource professionals, suitability
  as references, 78

I

Immigration Reform and Control Act, 16
Immunity laws, 21, 30–31
Industry-specific background checks, 22,
  26
Information
  benefits of providing, 7–8
  risks in not obtaining enough, 24–26
  risks in not providing enough, 22–24
  risks in obtaining too much, 26–29
  risks in providing too much, 14–22
Inquiries by rejected applicants, 86
Internal versus external screening. *See* Pre-
    employment screening firms
International issues, European perspective
  on legal issues in reference checking,
  32, 115–19
International laws, 32
Invasion of privacy, 21–22
Ireland, reference laws in, 116
Irwin, Michael, defamation case, 19

J

Job reference policy statement sample, 40

L

Ladder of reference inquiries, 79–80
Lawsuits and legal liability issues. *See also*
    State laws
  defamation concerns, 16–20

discrimination concerns, 14, 21, 26–29
employee consent and, 20–21, 40, 64–66
FCRA and, 29
inappropriate pre-employment inquiries,
28
invasion of privacy concerns, 21–22
misrepresentation concerns, 22–24
negligent hiring concerns, 24–26
qualified and absolute privileges, 19–20
reference checking dilemma, 11–13
retaliation concerns, 14–16
risk reduction, 7–8
risks in not obtaining enough
information, 24–26
risks in not providing enough
information, 22–24
risks in obtaining too much information,
26–29
risks in providing too much information,
14–22
test your knowledge, 12–13, 111–13
the truth and, 19
Libel, 16
Licenses, verifying, 55–56
Literacy problems, detection, 72

M
Medical conditions, disclosure, 21
"Miranda" warnings, 17
Misrepresentation, 22–24
Missouri, defamation case, 19
Motor vehicle record (MVR) checks, 59
MVR. *See* Motor vehicle record checks

N
"Name, rank, and serial number"
policy and approach to references,
17–19, 34–35, 53, 103
National Crime Information Center, 57–58
National Labor Relations Act, 16
Negligent hiring, 24–26. *See also* Lawsuits
and legal liability issues
Negligent referrals. *See* Misrepresentation
the Netherlands, reference laws in, 116
"No comment" policy and approach to
references, 19, 33–34, 103
"Non-check reference checks," 84–85
Notices, sample. *See* Forms, notices, and
policies, samples

O
Occupational Safety and Health Act, 16
Open-ended questions, 82–83
Oral communications, defamatory, 16
Outside agencies. *See* Pre-employment
screening firms
Outsourcing reference checking and
background screening, 5, 29. *See also*
Pre-employment screening firms

P
Personal information. *See* Confidential
information/confidentiality issues
Personal references, 74
Policies, sample. *See* Forms, notices, and
policies, samples
Policies and procedures. *See also* Reference
checking program
getting references, 60–63
giving references, 36–38
implementation of, 12
Pre-employment screening firms
client satisfaction, 97
compliance issues, 95
confidentiality issues, 95
cost considerations, 97
coverage issues, 96
FCRA and, 98–101
information accuracy issues, 96
internal versus external screening
considerations, 60, 91–95
sample listing, 121–23
selecting, 95–97
service options, 93–94
turnaround/completion time, 96–97
Pre-employment screening practices. *See
also* Getting references
extensive background investigations for
high-risk jobs, 56–60
inappropriate questions, 28
minimum requirements, 55–56
number of references to check, 56, 61
Preventing problems caused by poor hiring
decisions, 6–7
Privacy issues. *See* Confidential
information/confidentiality issues;
Invasion of privacy

Q

Qualified privilege, 19–20

R

Race Relations Act, 118
Reality check for the workplace, 8–10
Record keeping. *See* Documentation and record keeping
"Red flags" in completed applications, 64
Reference authorization form, 21, 39–40
Reference calls by telephone
about, 76
dealing with reluctant sources, 84–85
making the call, 80–83
Reference checking
about, 1–2, 4–5
centralizing, 77
challenges and opportunities, 5–8
internal versus external considerations, 60, 91–95. *See also* Pre-employment screening firms
legal liability risk reduction, 7–8. *See also* Lawsuits and legal liability issues
number of references to check, 56, 91
preventing problems caused by poor hiring decisions, 6–7
reality check for workplace, 8–10. *See also* Reference checking program
risks faced in failure to get truth, 3–4. *See also* Risks in reference checking
test your knowledge, 12–13, 111–13
Reference checking dilemma, 11–13
Reference checking form, 66–71
Reference checking program, 103–10
Reference firms and services. *See* Pre-employment screening firms
Rehabilitation Act of 1973, records retention, 87
Reid Psychological Systems survey, 6
Reluctant sources, 84–85
Retaliation, 14–16
Risks in reference checking
failure to get the truth, 3–4
not obtaining enough information, 24–26
obtaining too much information, 26–29
risks in not providing enough information, 22–24
risks in providing too much information, 14–22

Robinson, Charles, Sr., retaliation case, 15

S

Screening firms and services. *See* Pre-employment screening firms
Service letters laws, 22, 31–32
Shell Oil Company, retaliation case, 15
SHRM. *See* Society for Human Resource Management
Slander, 16
Social Security Number (SSN) verification, 59–60
Society for Human Resource Management (SHRM), v–vi
Society for Human Resource Management 1995 survey, contact methods, 76
Society for Human Resource Management 1998 survey
contact methods, 76
discovery of falsified information, 54
incidence of lawsuits, 11
number of references checked, 56
reference check statistics, 4–5
use of outside agencies, 53–54, 91
verification of former employers, 55
Society for Human Resource Management 1999 Workplace Violence Survey, 6
Spain, reference laws in, 116
Spring -v- Guardian Assurance plc., 117
SSN. *See* Social Security Number verification
State laws. *See also specific states*
blacklisting, 31, 32
credit check laws, FCRA and, 100–101
fair employment practices statutes, 16
immunity laws, 21, 30–31
liability for not disclosing known dangerous tendencies, 22
qualified privilege, 20
service letters, 31–32
Supervisors and managers, former
applicant reluctance to/refusal of contact, 74–75
evaluating references by, 85
suitability as references, 78
Sweden, reference laws in, 116

T

Telephone contacts. *See* Reference calls by telephone
Termination practices, giving references and, 41–42
Test your knowledge of legal issues, 12–13, 111–13
Title VII of the Civil Rights Act of 1964, 14, 16, 86
Tort claims, 16, 22–24
Trucking industry, special FCRA procedures, 100
Truth
  as absolute defense to defamation claim, 19
  employee dishonesty and theft, 6–7, 55
  "half-truths," 22–24
  Reid Psychological Systems survey results, 6
  verifying, 5–6

U

Uniformed Services Employment and Reemployment Rights Act, 16
United Kingdom, reference laws in, 116–19
U.S. Bankruptcy Code, 58
U.S. Chamber of Commerce, 6
U.S. Department of Justice, 6
U.S. Supreme Court, 15

V

Vietnam Era Veterans' Readjustment Assistance Act, records retention, 87
Violence in the workplace, 6

W

Wal-Mart Stores, Inc., defamation case, 19
Workplace issues
  sexual misconduct and harassment, 21
  violence and employee dishonesty, 6–7, 55
Workplace Violence Research Institute, 6
Written communications, defamatory, 16–17
Written reference contacts, 76

About the Author

Wendy Bliss is an attorney and Senior Professional in Human Resources (SPHR). As founder and principal of Bliss & Associates, she conducts seminars throughout the United States on issues, trends, and best practices in human resource management and employment law. Bliss & Associates, based in Colorado Springs, provides highly customized, in-house services in corporate training and executive coaching.

Bliss is a moderator and presenter for the Society for Human Resource Management's (SHRM's) HR Generalist certificate programs and has been a public seminar trainer for the American Management Association. She has spoken at national meetings of organizations including SHRM, the American Society for Training and Development, the Credit Union National Association, the Employment Law Institute, and the University of Phoenix.

She has commented on business and human resource questions for *ABC News* "20/20," CNN *Financial News*, *U.S. News & World Report*, *The New York Times*, the *San Francisco Examiner*, the *Associated Press*, and other national news media.

Bliss has been an adjunct faculty member at the University of Colorado at Colorado Springs and at the University of Phoenix, where she taught courses in human resources, employment law, organizational behavior, and business communications. She is the 2001 President of SHRM's Consultants Forum.

Selected Titles from the Society for Human Resource Management (SHRM®)

Solutions for Human Resource Managers, in printed and e-book formats

Supervisor's Guide to Labor Relations

Federal Employment Law: Volume I: *Understanding FMLA*

Federal Employment Law: Volume II: *Understanding COBRA*

Federal Employment Law: Volume III: *Preventing Harassment*

Federal Employment Law: Volume IV: *Understanding HIPAA*

To Order SHRM Books

SHRM offers a member discount on all books that it publishes or sells.
To order this or any other book published by the Society for Human Resource Management (SHRM®), contact the SHRMStore™.

Online: www.shrm.org/shrmstore
By Phone: 800-444-5006 (option #1); or 770-442-8633 (ext. 362);
   or TDD 703-548-6999
By Fax: 770-442-9742
By Mail: SHRM Distribution Center, P.O. Box 930132,
   Atlanta, GA 31193-0132, USA